W9-BLB-560

The everyday world at your fingertips

Spanish
picture dictionary

www.berlitzpublishing.com

Distribution
UK, Ireland and Europe:
Apa Publications (UK) Ltd;
sales@insightguides.com
United States and Canada:
Ingram Publisher Services;
ips@ingramcontent.com
Australia and New Zealand:
Woodslane; info@woodslane.com.au
Southeast Asia:
Apa Publications (SN) Pte;
singaporeoffice@insightguides.com
Hong Kong, Taiwan and China:
Apa Publications (HK) Ltd;
hongkongoffice@insightguides.com
Worldwide: Apa Publications (UK) Ltd;
sales@insightguides.com

**Special Sales, Content Licensing
and CoPublishing**
Insight Guides can be purchased in bulk
quantities at discounted prices. We can
create special editions, personalised
jackets and corporate imprints tailored to
your needs. sales@insightguides.com;
www.insightguides.biz

First Edition 2017

All Rights Reserved
© 2017 Apa Digital (CH) AG and
Apa Publications (UK) Ltd

Printed in China by CTPS

No part of this book may be reproduced,
stored in a retrieval system or transmitted
in any form or means electronic,
mechanical, photocopying, recording
or otherwise, without prior written
permission from Apa Publications.

Contact us
Every effort has been made to provide
accurate information in this publication,
but changes are inevitable. The publisher
cannot be responsible for any resulting
loss, inconvenience or injury. We would
appreciate it if readers would call our
attention to any errors or outdated
information. We also welcome your
suggestions; please contact us at:
berlitz@apaguide.co.uk

Berlitz Trademark Reg. U.S. Patent Office
and other countries. Marca Registrada.
Used under licence from the Berlitz
Investment Corporation

Series Editor: Carine Tracanelli
Editor: Berenika Wilczyńska
Head of Production: Rebeka Davies
Series design: Krzysztof Kop
Picture research & DTP design:
Tamkapress
English text: Carine Tracanelli &
Barbara Marchwica
Translation & simplified phonetics:
ILS AT
Photo credits: all Shutterstock and Fotolia

R0450243987

Introduction

Whether you are a total beginner or already have a sound knowledge of your chosen language, this Berlitz picture dictionary will help you to communicate quickly and easily. Packed with 2,000 useful terms, it covers all everyday situations, whether you're applying for a job, going shopping or just getting around. See, understand, memorise: visual learning by combining a word with an image helps you remember it more effectively as images affect us more than text alone.

To get the most out of your picture dictionary you can search for words in two ways: by theme (women's clothes, sporting facilities, hobbies, etc.) or by consulting the index at the end. You'll also find important phrases surrounding a topic in each chapter, ensuring that you have the foundations you need for communicating.

Each word is followed by its phonetic transcription to make sure you pronounce each word or sentence correctly. You will find a helpful guide to pronunciation in your chosen language on pages 7–10.

Note that the terms in this picture dictionary are always given in their singular form unless they are generally only used in their plural form, and all nouns are preceded by their gender-specific article. Certain terms are not gender-neutral and in such cases all genders are provided throughout in both the translation and phonetic transcription, ensuring you can communicate in all variants.

Berlitz are renowned for the quality and expertise of their language products. Discover the full range at www.berlitzpublishing.com.

Table of Contents

Pronunciation

This section is designed to make you familiar with the sounds of Spanish using our simplified phonetic transcription. You'll find the pronunciation of the Spanish letters and sounds explained below, together with their "imitated" equivalents. This system is used throughout the picture dictionary; simply read the pronunciation as if it were English, noting any special rules below.

Stress has been indicated in the phonetic pronunciation by capital letters.

If a word ends with n, s or a vowel the penultimate syllable is stressed, e.g.: **hacen** (AH-thehn), **sabes** (SAH-behs), **escuela** (ehs-KWEH-lah). If a word ends with a consonant other than n or s, the last syllable is stressed, e.g.: **amor** (ah-MOHR), **autoridad** (aw-toh-ree-THATH).

The rules above are not applied when a word has an accent mark. The acute accent ´ indicates stress, e.g. **río** (REE-yoh), **sesión** (seh-SYOHN).

Some Spanish words have more than one meaning. In these instances, the accent mark is also used to distinguish between them, e.g.: **él** (he) and **el** (the); **sí** (yes) and **si** (if).

There are some differences in vocabulary and pronunciation between the Spanish spoken in Spain and that in the Americas – although each is easily understood by the other. This picture dictionary uses the Spanish spoken in Spain.

PRONUNCIATION

Consonants

Letter(s)	Approximate Pronunciation	Symbol	Example	Pronunciation
b	1. as in English	b	**bueno**	BWEH-noh
	2. between vowels as in English, but softer	b	**bebida**	beh-BEE-dah
c	1. before e and i like th in *thin*	th	**centro**	THEHN-troh
	2. otherwise like k in *kit*	k	**como**	KOH-moh
ch	as in English	ch	**mucho**	MOO-choh
d	1. like d in *day*, but softer	d	**donde**	DOHN-deh
	2. between vowels and especially at the end of a word, like th in *thin*, but softer	th	**usted**	oos-TETH
g	1. before e and i, like ch in *Scottish loch*	kh	**urgente**	oor-KHEHN-teh
	2. elsewhere, like g in *get*	g	**ninguno**	neen-GOO-noh
h	always silent		**hombre**	OHM-breh
j	like ch in *Scottish loch*	kh	**bajo**	BAH-khoh
ll	like y in *yellow*	y	**lleno**	YEH-noh
ñ	like ni in *onion*	ny	**señor**	seh-NYOHR
q	like k in *kick*	k	**quince**	KEEN-theh
r	trilled	r	**puerto**	PWEHR-toh
r/rr	strongly trilled, usually single r at the beginning of a word and double rr	rr	**arriba**	ah-RREE-bah
s	like s in *same*	s	**sus**	soos
v	like b in *bad*, but softer	b	**viejo**	BYEH-khoh
z	like th in *thin*	th	**brazo**	BRAH-thoh

The letters f, k, l, m, n, p, t, w, x and y are pronounced approximately as in English.

Vowels

Letter(s)	Approximate Pronunciation	Symbol	Example	Pronunciation
a	like the a in *father*	ah	**gracias**	GRAH-thyahs
e	like e in *get*	eh	**esta**	EHS-tah
i	like ee in *meet*	ee	**sí**	see
o	like o in *rope*	oh	**dos**	dohs
u	1. like oo in *food*	oo	**uno**	OO-noh
	2. silent after g and q		**que**	keh
	3. when marked ü, like we in *well*	w	**antigüedad**	ahn-tee-gweh-THATH
y	1. like y in *yellow*	y	**hoy**	oy
	2. when alone, like ee in *meet*	ee	**y**	ee

Combined Vowels

Letter(s)	Approximate Pronunciation	Symbol	Example	Pronunciation
ai		ay	**aire**	AY-reh
au		aw	**causa**	KAW-sah
ei		ey	**aceite**	ah-THEY-teh
eu		ew	**euro**	EW-roh
oi		oy	**tiroides**	tee-ROY-dehs
ou		ow	**souvenir**	sow-veh-NEEHR
ia		ya	**piano**	PYAH-noh
ie		ye	**abierto**	ah-BYEHR-toh
io		yo	**varios**	BAH-ryohs

Letter(s)	Approximate Pronunciation	Symbol	Example	Pronunciation
iu		yoo	ciudad	thyoo-THATH
ua		wa	cuando	KWAHN-doh
ue		we	abuelo	ah-BWEH-loh
ui		wee	fui	fwee
uo		wo	antiguo	ahn-TEE-gwoh

A B C D E F G H I J K L M N
O P Q R S T U V W X Y Z

GENERAL VOCABULARY

first name
el nombre
ehl NOHM-breh

date of birth
la fecha de nacimiento
lah FEH-chah deh nah-thee-MYEHN-toh

place of birth
el lugar de nacimiento
ehl loo-GAHR deh nah-thee-MYEHN-toh

email address
la dirección de correo electrónico
lah dee-rek-THYOHN deh koh-RRE-oh eh-lek-TROH-nee-koh

phone number
el número de teléfono
ehl NOO-meh-roh deh teh-LEH-foh-noh

last name
el apellido
ehl ah-peh-YEE-thoh

age
la edad
lah eh-THATH

address	**la dirección**	lah dee-rek-THYOHN
marital status	**el estado civil**	ehl ehs-TAH-thoh thee-BEEL
children	**los niños**	lohs NEE-nyohs
home country	**el país de nacimiento**	ehl pa-EES deh nah-thee-MYEHN-toh
place of residence	**la residencia**	lah reh-see-DEHN-thyah
single	**soltero m / soltera f**	sohl-TEH-roh / sohl-TEH-rah
in a relationship	**en una relación**	ehn oo-NAH reh-lah-THYOHN
divorced	**divorciado m / divorciada f**	dee-bohr-THYAH-thoh / dee-bohr-THYAH-thah
married	**casado m / casada f**	kah-SAH-thoh / kah-SAH-thah
widowed	**viudo m / viuda f**	BYOO-thoh / BYOO-thah
What's your name?	**¿Cuál es su nombre?**	KWAHL ehs soo NOHM-breh?
Where are you from?	**¿De dónde es usted?**	deh DOHN-deh ehs oos-TEHTH?
Where were you born?	**¿Dónde nació?**	DOHN-deh nah-THYOH?
When were you born?	**¿Cuándo nació?**	KWAHN-doh nah-THYOH?
What is your address?	**¿Cuál es su dirección?**	KWAHL ehs soo dee-rek-THYOHN?
What's your phone number?	**¿Cuál es su número de teléfono?**	KWAHL ehs soo NOO-meh-roh deh teh-LEH-foh-noh?
Are you married?	**¿Está usted casado m / casada f?**	ehs-TAH oos-TEHTH kah-SAH-thoh / kah-SAH-thah?
Do you have children?	**¿Tiene hijos?**	TYEH-neh EE-khos?

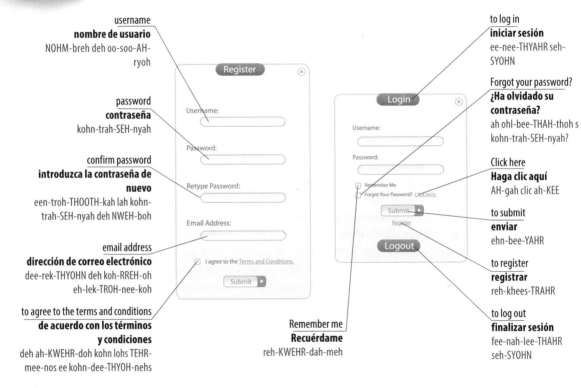

username
nombre de usuario
NOHM-breh deh oo-soo-AH-ryoh

password
contraseña
kohn-trah-SEH-nyah

confirm password
introduzca la contraseña de nuevo
een-troh-THOOTH-kah lah kohn-trah-SEH-nyah deh NWEH-boh

email address
dirección de correo electrónico
dee-rek-THYOHN deh koh-RREH-oh eh-lek-TROH-nee-koh

to agree to the terms and conditions
de acuerdo con los términos y condiciones
deh ah-KWEHR-doh kohn lohs TEHR-mee-nos ee kohn-dee-THYOH-nehs

to log in
iniciar sesión
ee-nee-THYAHR seh-SYOHN

Forgot your password?
¿Ha olvidado su contraseña?
ah ohl-bee-THAH-thoh s kohn-trah-SEH-nyah?

Click here
Haga clic aquí
AH-gah clic ah-KEE

to submit
enviar
ehn-bee-YAHR

to register
registrar
reh-khees-TRAHR

to log out
finalizar sesión
fee-nah-lee-THAHR seh-SYOHN

Remember me
Recuérdame
reh-KWEHR-dah-meh

0 1 2 3 4 5 6 7 8 9

0	zero	**cero**	THEH-roh
1	one	**uno**	OO-noh
2	two	**dos**	dohs
3	three	**tres**	trehs
4	four	**cuatro**	KWAH-troh
5	five	**cinco**	THEEN-koh
6	six	**seis**	seyhs
7	seven	**siete**	SYEH-teh
8	eight	**ocho**	OH-choh
9	nine	**nueve**	NWEH-beh
10	ten	**diez**	dyeth
11	eleven	**once**	OHN-theh
12	twelve	**doce**	DOH-theh
13	thirteen	**trece**	TREH-theh
14	fourteen	**catorce**	kah-TOHR-theh
15	fifteen	**quince**	KEEN-theh
16	sixteen	**dieciséis**	dyeh-thee-SEYS

17	seventeen	**diecisiete**	dyeh-thee-SYEH-teh
18	eighteen	**dieciocho**	dyeh-thee-OH-choh
19	nineteen	**diecinueve**	dyeh-thee-NWEH-beh
20	twenty	**veinte**	BEYHN-teh
21	twenty-one	**veintiuno**	BEYHN-tee-OO-noh
30	thirty	**treinta**	TREYHN-tah
40	forty	**cuarenta**	kwah-REHN-tah
50	fifty	**cincuenta**	theen-KWEN-tah
60	sixty	**sesenta**	seh-SEHN-tah
70	seventy	**setenta**	seh-TEHN-tah
80	eighty	**ochenta**	oh-CHEN-tah
90	ninety	**noventa**	noh-BEHN-tah
100	one hundred	**cien**	thyehn
101	one hundred and one	**ciento uno**	THYEHN-toh OO-noh
1000	one thousand	**mil**	meel
1 000 000	one million	**un millón**	oon mee-YOHN

1st (first)
el primero
el pree-MEH-roh

2nd (second)
el segundo
el seh-GOON-doh

3rd (third)
el tercero
el tehr-THEH-roh

4th	fourth	**el cuarto**	ehl KWAHR-toh
5th	fifth	**el quinto**	ehl KEEN-toh
6th	sixth	**el sexto**	ehl SEX-toh
7th	seventh	**el séptimo**	ehl SEHP-tee-moh
8th	eighth	**el octavo**	ehl ohk-TAH-boh
9th	ninth	**el noveno**	ehl noh-BEH-noh
10th	tenth	**el décimo**	ehl DEH-thee-moh
11th	eleventh	**el undécimo**	ehl oon-DEH-thee-moh

12th	twelfth	**el duodécimo**	ehl doo-oh-THEH-thee-moh
13th	thirteenth	**el decimotercero**	ehl deh-thee-moh-tehr-THE-roh
14th	fourteenth	**el decimocuarto**	ehl deh-thee-moh-KWAHR-toh
15th	fifteenth	**el decimoquinto**	ehl deh-thee-moh-KEEN-toh
16th	sixteenth	**el decimosexto**	ehl deh-thee-moh-SEX-toh
17th	seventeenth	**el decimoséptimo**	ehl deh-thee-moh-SEHP-tee-moh
18th	eighteenth	**el decimoctavo**	ehl deh-thee-mohk-TAH-boh
19th	nineteenth	**el decimonoveno**	ehl deh-thee-moh-noh-BEH-noh
20th	twentieth	**el vigésimo**	ehl bee-KHEH-see-moh
21st	twenty-first	**el vigésimo primero**	ehl bee-KHEH-see-moh pree-MEH-roh
22nd	twenty-second	**el vigésimo segundo**	ehl bee-KHEH-see-moh seh-GOON-doh
23rd	twenty-third	**el vigésimo tercero**	ehl bee-KHEH-see-moh tehr-THEH-roh
24th	twenty-fourth	**el vigésimo cuarto**	ehl bee-KHEH-see-moh KWAHR-toh
25th	twenty-fifth	**el vigésimo quinto**	ehl bee-KHEH-see-moh KEEN-toh
26th	twenty-sixth	**el vigésimo sexto**	ehl bee-KHEH-see-moh SEX-toh
27th	twenty-seventh	**el vigésimo séptimo**	ehl bee-KHEH-see-moh SEHP-tee-moh
28th	twenty-eighth	**el vigésimo octavo**	ehl bee-KHEH-see-moh ohk-TAH-boh
29th	twenty-ninth	**el vigésimo noveno**	ehl bee-KHEH-see-moh noh-BEH-noh
30th	thirtieth	**el trigésimo**	ehl tree-KHEH-see-moh
40th	fortieth	**el cuadragésimo**	ehl kwah-drah-KHEH-see-moh
50th	fiftieth	**el quincuagésimo**	ehl keen-kwah-KHEH-see-moh
60th	sixtieth	**el sexagésimo**	ehl sex-ah-KHEH-see-moh
70th	seventieth	**el septuagésimo**	ehl sehp-too-ah-KHEH-see-moh
80th	eightieth	**el octogésimo**	ehl ohk-toh-KHEH-see-moh
90th	ninetieth	**el nonagésimo**	ehl noh-nah-KHEH-see-moh
100th	hundredth	**el centésimo**	ehl then-TEH-see-moh

noon	**el mediodía**	ehl meh-thyoh-THEE-yah
midnight	**la medianoche**	lah meh-thyah-NOH-cheh

one am	**la una**	lah OO-nah
one pm	**las trece**	lahs TREH-theh

two am	**las dos**	lahs dohs
two pm	**las catorce**	lahs kah-TOHR-theh

three am	**las tres**	lahs trehs
three pm	**las quince**	lahs KEEN-theh

four am	**las cuatro**	lahs KWAH-troh
four pm	**las dieciséis**	lahs dyeh-thee-SEYS

five am	**las cinco**	lahs THEEN-koh
five pm	**las diecisiete**	lahs dyeh-thee-SYEH-teh

six am	**las seis**	lahs seyhs
six pm	**las dieciocho**	lahs dyeh-thee-OH-choh

seven am	**las siete**	lahs SYEH-teh
seven pm	**las diecinueve**	lahs dyeh-thee-NWEH-beh

eight am	**las ocho**	lahs OH-choh
eight pm	**las veinte**	lahs BEYHN-teh

nine am	**las nueve**	lahs NWEH-beh
nine pm	**las veintiuno**	lahs beyhn-tee-OO-noh

ten am	**las diez**	lahs dyeth
ten pm	**las veintidós**	lahs beyhn-tee-DOHS

eleven am	**las once**	lahs OHN-theh
eleven pm	**las veintitrés**	lahs beyhn-tee-TREHS

quarter to
menos cuarto
MEH-nohs KWAHR-toh

ten to
menos diez
MEH-nohs DYETH

five to
menos cinco
MEH-nohs THEEN-koh

... o'clock
la hora
lah OH-rah

five past
y cinco
ee THEEN-koh

ten past
y diez
ee dyeth

quarter past
y cuarto
ee KWAHR-toh

half past
y media
ee MEH-thyah

What time is it?	**¿Qué hora es?**	KEH OH-rah ehs?
It's nine thirty.	**Son las nueve y media.**	sohn lahs NWEH-beh ee MEH-thyah
Excuse me, could you tell me the time please?	**¿Perdone, podría decirme la hora por favor?**	pehr-DOH-neh, pod-REE-ya deh-THEER-meh lah OH-rah pohr fah-BOHR?
It's about half past nine.	**Son sobre las nueve y media.**	SOHN soh-breh lahs NWEH-beh ee MEH-thyah

Monday
lunes
LOO-nes

Tuesday
martes
MAHR-tehs

Wednesday
miércoles
MYEHR-koh-lehs

Thursday
jueves
KHWEH-behs

Friday
viernes
BYEHR-nehs

Saturday
sábado
SAH-bah-thoh

Sunday
domingo
doh-MEEN-goh

on Monday	**el lunes**	ehl LOO-nes
from Tuesday	**desde el martes**	DEHS-deh ehl MAHR-tehs
until Wednesday	**hasta el miércoles**	AH-stah ehl MYEHR-koh-lehs

JANUARY

January
enero
eh-NEH-roh

FEBRUARY

February
febrero
feb-REH-roh

MARCH

March
marzo
MAHR-thoh

APRIL

April
abril
ahb-REEL

MAY

May
mayo
MAH-yoh

JUNE

June
junio
KHOO-nyoh

JULY

July
julio
KHOO-lyoh

AUGUST

August
agosto
ah-GOH-stoh

SEPTEMBER

September
septiembre
sep-TYEHM-breh

OCTOBER

October
octubre
ohk-TOO-breh

NOVEMBER

November
noviembre
noh-BYEHM-breh

DECEMBER

December
diciembre
dee-THYEHM-breh

in July	**en julio**	ehn KHOO-lyoh
since September	**desde septiembre**	DEHS-deh sep-TYEHM-breh
until October	**hasta octubre**	AH-stah ohk-TOO-breh
for two months	**durante dos meses**	doo-RAHN-teh dohs MEH-sehs

morning	late morning	noon	afternoon	evening	night
la mañana	**antes del mediodía**	**el mediodía**	**la tarde**	**la noche**	**la noche**
lah mah-NYAH-nah	AHN-tehs dehl meh-thyoh-THEE-yah	ehl meh-thyoh-THEE-yah	lah TAHR-deh	lah NOH-cheh	lah NOH-cheh

in the morning	**por la mañana**	pohr lah mah-NYAH-nah
in the evening	**por la tarde**	pohr lah TAHR-deh
in the night	**por la noche**	pohr lah NOH-cheh

ATM / cashpoint
el cajero
el kah-KHEH-roh

cash
el dinero en efectivo
ehl dee-NEH-roh ehn
eh-feh-KTEE-boh

bank statement
el extracto de cuenta
el ex-TRAH-ktoh deh KWEHN-tah

cheque
el cheque
el CHEH-keh

account	**la cuenta**	lah KWEHN-tah
bank	**el banco**	ehl BAHN-koh
bank charges	**los gastos bancarios**	lohs GAHS-tohs bahn-KAH-ryohs
debit card	**la tarjeta de débito**	lah tahr-KHEH-tah deh DEH-bee-toh
debt	**la deuda**	lah DEHW-dah
current account	**la cuenta corriente**	lah KWEHN-tah koh-RYEHN-teh
loan	**el préstamo**	ehl PREH-stah-moh
mortgage	**la hipoteca**	lah ee-poh-TEH-kah
savings account	**la cuenta de ahorros**	lah KWEHN-tah deh ah-OH-rrohs
standing order	**la orden permanente**	lah OHR-dehn pehr-mah-NEHN-teh
to borrow money	**pedir dinero prestado**	peh-THEER dee-NEH-roh preh-STAH-thoh
to invest	**invertir**	een-behr-TEER
to lend money	**prestar dinero**	prehs-TAHR dee-NEH-roh
to pay	**pagar**	pah-GAHR
to take out a loan	**pedir un préstamo**	peh-THEER oon PREH-stah-moh
to withdraw from the account	**retirar de la cuenta**	rreh-tee-RAHR deh lah KWEHN-tah
to take out a mortgage	**pedir una hipoteca**	peh-THEER OO-nah ee-poh-TEH-kah
to withdraw	**retirar efectivo**	rreh-tee-RAHR eh-feh-KTEE-boh

credit card
la tarjeta de crédito
lah tahr-KHEH-tah deh KREH-thee-toh

to save
ahorrar
ah-oh-RRAHR

23

Pound Sterling
la libra esterlina
lah LEE-brah
ehs-tehr-LEE-nah

Euro
el euro
ehl EHW-roh

Dollar
el dólar
ehl DOH-lahr

Franc
el franco
ehl FRAHN-koh

Yen
el yen
ehl yehn

Won
el won
ehl wohn

Yuan
el yuan
ehl YOO-ahn

Indian Rupee
la rupia india
lah RROO-pyah
EEN-dyah

Zloty
el zloty
ehl THLOH-tee

Ruble
el rublo
ehl RROOB-loh

Leu
el leu
ehl lehw

Forint
el forinto
ehl foh-REEN-toh

Krone	**la corona**	lah koh-ROH-nah
Peso	**el peso**	ehl PEH-soh
Pound	**la libra**	lah LEEB-rah
Dinar	**el dinar**	ehl dee-NAHR
Shilling	**el chelín**	ehl cheh-LEEN
Dirham	**el dirham**	ehl DEER-ahm
Rial	**el rial**	ehl rree-AHL
Dong	**el dong**	ehl dohn

exchange rate	**el tipo de cambio**	ehl TEE-poh deh KAHM-byoh
exchange rate for US Dollars to Japanese Yen	**la tasa de cambio de dólares estadounidenses a yenes japoneses**	lah TAH-sah deh KAHM-byoh deh DOH-lah-rehs ehs-TAH-thoh-oo-nee-THEN-sehs ah YEH-nehs khah-poh-NEH-sehs
foreign exchange	**el intercambio de divisa**	ehl een-tehr-KAHM-byoh deh dee-BEE-sah
foreign exchange rate	**el tipo de cambio**	ehl TEE-poh deh KAHM-byoh

PEOPLE

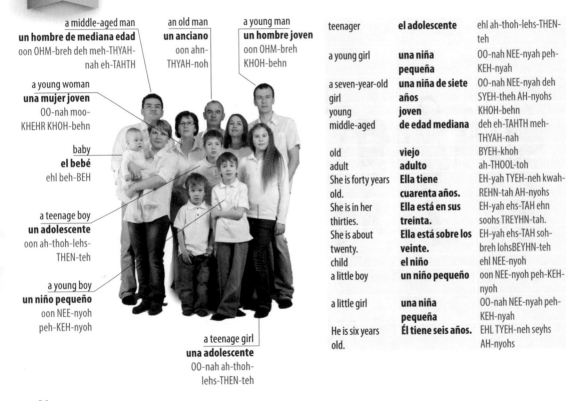

a middle-aged man
un hombre de mediana edad
oon OHM-breh deh meh-THYAH-nah eh-TAHTH

an old man
un anciano
oon ahn-THYAH-noh

a young man
un hombre joven
oon OHM-breh KHOH-behn

a young woman
una mujer joven
OO-nah moo-KHEHR KHOH-behn

baby
el bebé
ehl beh-BEH

a teenage boy
un adolescente
oon ah-thoh-lehs-THEN-teh

a young boy
un niño pequeño
oon NEE-nyoh peh-KEH-nyoh

a teenage girl
una adolescente
OO-nah ah-thoh-lehs-THEN-teh

teenager	**el adolescente**	ehl ah-thoh-lehs-THEN-teh
a young girl	**una niña pequeña**	OO-nah NEE-nyah peh-KEH-nyah
a seven-year-old girl	**una niña de siete años**	OO-nah NEE-nyah deh SYEH-theh AH-nyohs
young	**joven**	KHOH-behn
middle-aged	**de edad mediana**	deh eh-TAHTH meh-THYAH-nah
old	**viejo**	BYEH-khoh
adult	**adulto**	ah-THOOL-toh
She is forty years old.	**Ella tiene cuarenta años.**	EH-yah TYEH-neh kwah-REHN-tah AH-nyohs
She is in her thirties.	**Ella está en sus treinta.**	EH-yah ehs-TAH ehn soohs TREYHN-tah.
She is about twenty.	**Ella está sobre los veinte.**	EH-yah ehs-TAH soh-breh lohs BEYHN-teh
child	**el niño**	ehl NEE-nyoh
a little boy	**un niño pequeño**	oon NEE-nyoh peh-KEH-nyoh
a little girl	**una niña pequeña**	OO-nah NEE-nyah peh-KEH-nyah
He is six years old.	**Él tiene seis años.**	EHL TYEH-neh seyhs AH-nyohs

a beautiful girl
un niña guapa
OO-nah NEE-nyah GWAH-pah

a pretty woman
una mujer bella
OO-nah moo-KHEHR BEH-yah

a handsome man
un hombre guapo
oon OHM-breh GWAH-poh

attractive	**atractivo**	ah-trahk-TEE-boh
beautiful	**guapo**	GWAH-poh
cute	**lindo**	LEEN-doh
handsome	**guapo**	GWAH-poh
ugly	**feo**	FEH-oh
unattractive	**poco atractivo**	POH-koh ah-trahk-TEE-boh
casually dressed	**vestido casualmente**	beh-STEE-thoh kah-soo-ahl-MEHN-teh

dirty	**sucio**	SOO-thyoh
elegant	**elegante**	eh-leh-GAHN-teh
pretty	**bonito**	boh-NEE-toh
fashionable	**a la moda**	ah lah MOH-thah
neat	**ordenado**	ohr-deh-NAH-thoh
poorly dressed	**mal vestido**	mahl behs-TEE-thoh
untidy	**desordenado**	deh-sohr-deh-NAH-thoh
well-dressed	**bien vestido**	byehn behs-TEE-thoh

She is taller than him.	**Ella es más alta que él.**	EH-yah ehs mahs AHL-tah keh EHL
He isn't as tall as her.	**Él no es tan alto como ella.**	EHL noh ehs tahn AHL-toh KOH-moh EH-yah
She is of average height.	**Ella es de estatura media.**	EH-yah ehs deh eh-stah-TOO-rah MEH-thyah

very tall	tall	quite tall	not very tall	short
muy alto	**alto**	**bastante alto**	**no muy alto**	**bajo**
mooy AHL-toh	AHL-toh	bah-STAHN-teh AHL-toh	noh mooy AHL-toh	BAH-khoh

thin	slim	plump	fat
delgado	**delgado**	**rechoncho**	**gordo**
del-GAH-thoh	del-GAH-thoh	reh-CHOHN-choh	GOHR-doh

slender	**esbelto**	ehs-BEHL-toh
skinny	**flaco**	FLAH-koh
obese	**obeso**	oh-BEH-soh
underweight	**bajo peso**	BAH-khoh PEH-soh
overweight	**sobrepeso**	soh-breh-PEH-soh
She is overweight / underweight.	**Tiene sobrepeso / bajo peso.**	TYEH-neh soh-breh-PEH-soh / BAH-khoh PEH-soh.
to lose weight	**perder peso**	pehr-DEHR PEH-soh

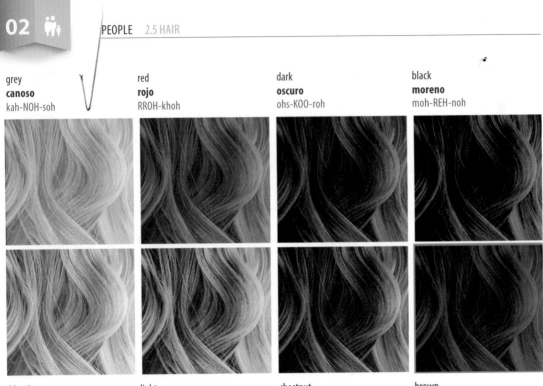

grey
canoso
kah-NOH-soh

red
rojo
RROH-khoh

dark
oscuro
ohs-KOO-roh

black
moreno
moh-REH-noh

blond
rubio
RROO-byoh

light
claro
KLAH-roh

chestnut
castaño
kahs-TAH-nyoh

brown
castaño
kas-TAH-nee-oh

straight
liso
LEE-soh

curly
rizado
rree-THAH-thoh

wavy
ondulado
ohn-doo-LAH-thoh

thick
espeso
ehs-PEH-soh

bald
calvo
KAHL-boh

long
largo
LAHR-goh

short
corto
KOHR-toh

shoulder-length
hasta el hombro
AH-stah ehl OHM-broh

medium-length
de longitud media
deh lohn-khee-TOOTH
MEH-thyah

a brunette	**una morena**	OO-nah moh-REH-nah
a redhead	**una pelirroja**	OO-nah peh-lee-RROH-khah
a blonde	**una rubia**	OO-nah RROO-byah
a dark-haired woman	**una mujer de pelo oscuro**	OO-nah moo-KHEHR deh PEH-loh ohs-KOO-roh
He has long dark hair.	**Él tiene el pelo largo y oscuro.**	EHL TYEH-neh ehl PEH-loh LAHR-goh ee ohs-KOO-roh
He has curly hair.	**Él tiene el pelo rizado.**	EHL TYEH-neh ehl PEH-loh rree-THAH-thoh.
He is bald.	**Él está calvo.**	EHL ehs-TAH KAHL-boh

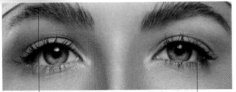

eyebrows	eyelashes
las cejas	**las pestañas**
lahs THEH-khahs	lahs pehs-TAH-nyahs

glasses
las gafas
lahs GAH-fahs

sunglasses
las gafas de sol
lahs GAH-fahs deh sohl

blue	**azules**	ah-THOO-lehs
grey	**grises**	GREE-sehs
green	**verdes**	BEHR-dehs
brown	**marrones**	mah-RROH-nehs
dark	**oscuros**	ohs-KOO-rohs
light	**claros**	KLAH-rohs

short sighted	**miope**	MYOH-peh
blind	**ciego**	THYEH-goh
She wears glasses.	**Ella lleva gafas.**	EH-yah YEH-bah GAH-fahs
She has blue eyes.	**Ella tiene los ojos azules.**	EH-yah TYEH-neh lohs OH-khohs ah-THOO-lehs
His eyes are dark brown.	**Sus ojos son de color marrón oscuro.**	soos OH-khohs sohn deh koh-LOHR mah-RROHN ohs-KOO-roh

beige	**beige**	beys
blue	**azul**	ah-THOOL
brown	**marrón**	mah-RROHN
dark blue	**azul oscuro**	ah-THOOL ohs-KOO-roh
yellow	**amarillo**	ah-mah-REE-yoh
grey	**gris**	grees
green	**verde**	BEHR-deh
light blue	**azul claro**	ah-THOOL KLAH-roh
lilac	**lila**	LEE-lah
orange	**naranja**	nah-RAHN-khah
pink	**rosado**	rroh-SAH-thoh
red	**rojo**	RROH-khoh
black	**negro**	NEH-groh
turquoise	**turquesa**	toor-KEH-sah
violet	**violeta**	byoh-LEH-tah
white	**blanco**	BLAHN-koh
gold	**oro**	OH-roh
silver	**plata**	PLAH-tah

positive
positivo
poh-see-TEE-boh

stubborn
obstinado
ohb-stee-NAH-thoh

lucky
afortunado
ah-fohr-too-NAH-thoh

dreamer
soñador
soh-nyah-THOHR

visionary
visionario
bee-syoh-NAH-ryoh

funny
gracioso
grah-THYOH-soh

talkative
hablador
ah-blah-THOHR

energetic
enérgico
eh-NEHR-khee-koh

negative
negativo
neh-gah-TEE-boh

creative	**creativo**	kreh-ah-TEE-boh
adventurous	**aventurero**	ah-behn-too-REH-roh
kind	**amable**	ah-MAH-bleh
calm	**tranquilo**	trahn-KEE-loh
caring	**cariñoso**	kah-ree-NYOH-soh
punctual	**puntual**	poon-too-WAHL
crazy	**loco**	LOH-koh
liar	**mentiroso**	mehn-tee-ROH-soh
frank	**sincero**	theen-THEH-roh
strong	**fuerte**	FWEHR-teh

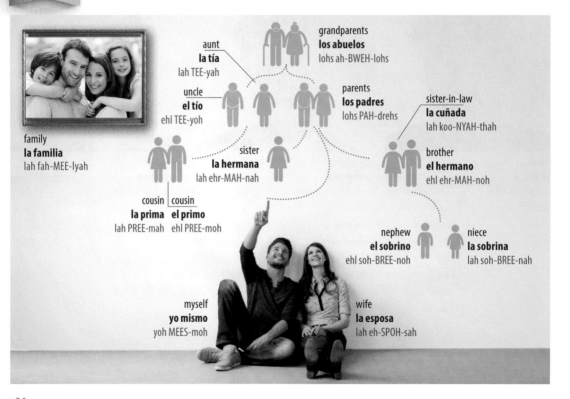

grandparents
los abuelos
lohs ah-BWEH-lohs

aunt
la tía
lah TEE-yah

uncle
el tío
ehl TEE-yoh

parents
los padres
lohs PAH-drehs

sister-in-law
la cuñada
lah koo-NYAH-thah

family
la familia
lah fah-MEE-lyah

sister
la hermana
lah ehr-MAH-nah

brother
el hermano
ehl ehr-MAH-noh

cousin
la prima
lah PREE-mah

cousin
el primo
ehl PREE-moh

nephew
el sobrino
ehl soh-BREE-noh

niece
la sobrina
lah soh-BREE-nah

myself
yo mismo
yoh MEES-moh

wife
la esposa
lah eh-SPOH-sah

grandchildren	**los nietos**	lohs NYEH-tohs
daughter	**la hija**	lah EE-khah
father	**el padre**	ehl PAH-dreh
father-in-law	**el suegro**	ehl SWEH-groh
grandchild	**el nieto**	ehl NYEH-toh
granddaughter	**la nieta**	lah NYEH-tah
grandson	**el nieto**	ehl NYEH-toh
grandfather	**el abuelo**	ehl ah-BWEH-loh
grandmother	**la abuela**	lah ah-BWEH-lah
great-grandparents	**los bisabuelos**	lohs bee-sah-BWEH-lohs
husband	**el marido**	ehl mah-REE-thoh
mother	**la madre**	lah MAH-dreh
mother-in-law	**la suegra**	lah SWEH-grah
son	**el hijo**	ehl EE-khoh
twin brother	**el hermano gemelo**	ehl ehr-MAH-noh kheh-MEH-loh
brother-in-law	**el cuñado**	ehl koo-NYAH-thoh

single child
el hijo único / la hija única
ehl EE-khoh OO-nee-koh / lah EE-khah OO-nee-kah

family with two children
la familia con dos hijos
lah fah-MEE-lyah kohn dohs EE-khohs

big family
la familia numerosa
lah fah-MEE-lyah noo-meh-ROH-sah

childless
sin hijos
seen EE-khohs

single father
el padre soltero
ehl PAH-dreh sohl-TEH-roh

single mother
la madre soltera
lah MAH-dreh sohl-TEH-rah

adoption
la adopción
lah ah-thop-THYOHN

orphan
el huérfano *m* / la huérfana *f*
ehl WEHR-fah-noh / lah WEHR-fah-nah

widow
viuda
BYOO-thah

stepfather	**el padrastro**	pah-DRAHS-troh		to be engaged	**comprometerse**	kohm-proh-meh-TEHR-seh
stepmother	**la madrastra**	mah-DRAHS-trah		to marry	**casarse**	kah-SAHR-seh
to be pregnant	**estar embarazada**	ehs-TAHR ehm-bah-rah-THAH-thah		to be married to	**estar casado *m* / casada con *f***	ehs-TAHR kah-SAH-thoh / kah-SAH-thah cohn
to expect a baby	**esperar un bebé**	ehs-peh-RAHR oon beh-BEH		divorced	**divorciado *m* / divorciada *f***	dee-bohr-THYAH-thoh / dee-bohr-THYAH-thah
to give birth to	**dar a luz**	dahr ah LOOTH				
born	**nacido *m* / nacida *f***	nah-THEE-thoh / nah-THEE-thah		widowed	**viudo *m* / viuda *f***	BYOO-thoh / BYOO-thah
to baptise	**bautizar**	bahw-tee-THAHR		widower	**viudo**	BYOO-thoh
to raise	**educar**	eh-thoo-KAHR		to die	**morir**	moh-REER

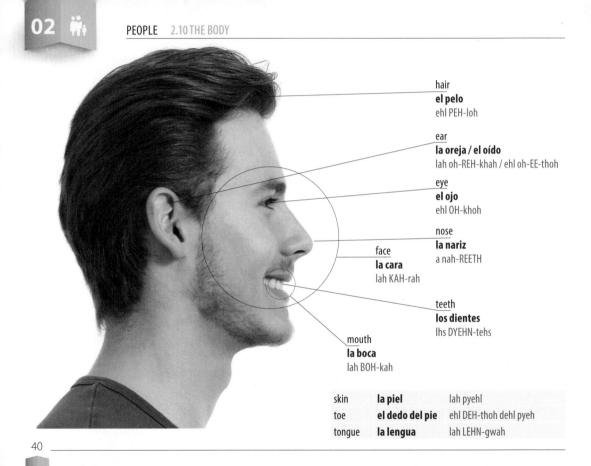

hair
el pelo
ehl PEH-loh

ear
la oreja / el oído
lah oh-REH-khah / ehl oh-EE-thoh

eye
el ojo
ehl OH-khoh

nose
la nariz
a nah-REETH

face
la cara
lah KAH-rah

teeth
los dientes
lhs DYEHN-tehs

mouth
la boca
lah BOH-kah

skin	**la piel**	lah pyehl
toe	**el dedo del pie**	ehl DEH-thoh dehl pyeh
tongue	**la lengua**	lah LEHN-gwah

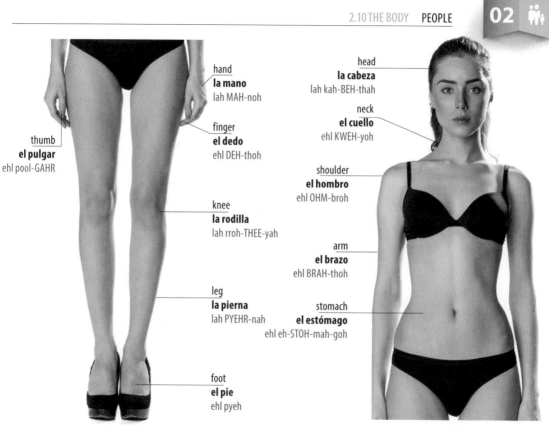

hand
la mano
lah MAH-noh

head
la cabeza
lah kah-BEH-thah

finger
el dedo
ehl DEH-thoh

neck
el cuello
ehl KWEH-yoh

thumb
el pulgar
ehl pool-GAHR

shoulder
el hombro
ehl OHM-broh

knee
la rodilla
lah rroh-THEE-yah

arm
el brazo
ehl BRAH-thoh

leg
la pierna
lah PYEHR-nah

stomach
el estómago
ehl eh-STOH-mah-goh

foot
el pie
ehl pyeh

angry
enfadado
ehn-fah-THAH-thoh

annoyed
molesto
moh-LEH-stoh

ashamed
avergonzado
ah-behr-gohn-THAH-thoh

betrayed
traicionado
trah-ee-THYOH-nah-thoh

confused
confundido
kohn-foon-DEE-thoh

confident
seguro
seh-GOO-roh

cheated
engañado
ehn-gah-NYAH-thoh

depressed
deprimido
deh-pree-MEE-thoh

delighted
encantando
ehn-kahn-TAH-thoh

disappointed
decepcionado
deh-thep-thyoh-NAH-tho

excited
entusiasmado
ehn-too-syahs-MAH-thoh

embarrassed
avergonzado
ah-behr-gohn-THAH-thoh

furious
furioso
foo-RYOH-soh

frightened
asustado
ah-soos-TAH-thoh

happy
feliz
feh-LEETH

horrified
horrorizado
ohr-roh-ree-THAH-thoh

irritated
irritado
eer-ree-TAH-thoh

intrigued
intrigado
een-tree-GAH-thoh

jealous
celoso
theh-LOH-soh

lazy
perezoso
peh-reh-THOH-soh

lucky
afortunado
ah-fohr-too-NAH-thoh

relaxed
relajado
rreh-lah-KHAH-thoh

sad
triste
TREE-steh

stressed
estresado
ehs-treh-SAH-thoh

terrified
aterrorizado
ah-tehr-roh-ree-THAH-thoh

upset
molesto
moh-LEH-stoh

unhappy
infeliz
een-feh-LEETH

| hobby **el hobby** ehl OHB-bee | My hobby is … Are you interested in …? | **Mi hobby es …** **¿Está interesado en …?** | mee OHB-bee ehs … ehs-TAHS een-teh-reh-SAH-thoh ehn … |

baking
hornear
ohr-neh-AHR

coin collecting
el coleccionismo de monedas
ehl koh-lehk-thyoh-NEE-smoh
deh moh-NEH-thas

woodworking
el trabajo de la madera
ehl trah-BAH-khoh deh lah
mah-THEH-rah

stamp collecting
la filatelia
lah fee-lah-TEH-lyah

cooking
la cocina
lah koh-THEE-nah

dance
el baile
ehl BY-leh

drawing
el dibujo
ehl dee-BOO-khoh

reading
la lectura
lah lehk-TOO-rah

jewellery making
la elaboración de joyas
lah eh-lah-boh-rah-THYOHN
deh KHOH-yahs

knitting
el tejido de punto
ehl teh-KHEE-thoh deh POON-toh

painting
la pintura
lah peen-TOO-rah

sewing
la costura
lah kohs-TOO-rah

badminton
el bádminton
ehl BAHD-meen-tohn

bowling
los bolos
lohs BOH-lohs

boxing
el boxeo
ehl boh-XEH-oh

chess
el ajedrez
ehl ah-kheh-DRETH

cycling
el ciclismo
ehl thee-KLEE-smoh

darts
los dardos
lohs DAHR-dohs

diving
el buceo
ehl boo-THEH-oh

fishing
la pesca
lah PEHS-kah

football
el fútbol
ehl FOOT-bohl

orienteering
la orientación
lah oh-ryehn-tah-THYOHN

gymnastics
la gimnasia
lah kheem-NAH-syah

handball
el balonmano
ehl bah-lohn-MAH-noh

jogging
el jogging
ehl YOH-kheen

kayaking
el kayak
ehl KAH-yahk

martial arts
las artes marciales
lahs AHR-tehs mahr-THYAH-lehs

mountain biking
la bicicleta de montaña
lah bee-thee-KLEH-tah deh mohn-TAH-nyah

paintball
el paintball
ehl PEYN-bohl

photography
la fotografía
lah foh-toh-grah-FEE-yah

rock climbing
la escalada en roca
lah ehs-kah-LAH-thah ehn RROH-kah

running
el jogging
ehl YOH-kheen

sailing
la navegación
lah nah-beh-gah-THYOHN

surfing
el surf
ehl soorf

swimming
la natación
lah nah-tah-THYOHN

table tennis
el tenis de mesa
ehl TEH-nees deh MEH-sah

travel
los viajes
lohs BYAH-khes

tennis
el tenis
ehl TEH-nees

yoga
el yoga
ehl YOH-gah

I like to swim.	**Me gusta nadar.**	meh GOO-stah nah-THAHR
What activities do you like to do?	**¿Qué le gusta hacer?**	KEH teh GOO-stah ah-THEHR?

to get up
levantarse
leh-bahn-TAHR-seh

to take a shower
ducharse
doo-CHAHR-seh

to brush your teeth
cepillarse los dientes
theh-pee-YAHR-seh lohs DYEHN-tehs

to floss your teeth
usar hilo dental
oo-SAHR EE-loh dehn-TAHL

to shave
afeitarse
ah-fey-TAHR-seh

to brush your hair
cepillarse el pelo
theh-pee-YAHR-seh ehl PEH-loh

49

to put on makeup
ponerse maquillaje
poh-NEHR-seh mah-kee-YAH-kheh

to get dressed
vestirse
beh-STEER-seh

to get undressed
desvestirse
dehs-beh-STEER-seh

to take a bath
bañarse
bah-NYAHR-seh

to go to bed
irse a la cama
EER-seh ah lah KAH-mah

to sleep
dormir
dohr-MEER

Valentine's Day
el Día de San Valentín
ehl DEE-yah deh sahn
bah-lehn-TEEN

graduation
la graduación
lah grah-doo-ah-THYOHN

Easter
la Pascua
PAHS-kwah

engagement
el compromiso
ehl kohm-proh-MEE-soh

marriage
el matrimonio
ehl mah-tree-MOH-nyoh

bride
la novia
lah NOH-byah

Christmas
la Navidad
lah nah-bee-THATH

51

Santa Claus / Father Christmas
Papá Noel
pah-PAH noh-EHL

52

candle
la vela
lah BEH-lah

present / gift
el regalo
ehl rreh-GAH-loh

Advent calendar
el Calendario de Adviento
ehl kha-lehn-DAH-ryoh deh
ahd-BYEHN-toh

decoration
la decoración
lah deh-koh-rah-THYON

champagne
el champán
ehl chahm-PAHN

party
la fiesta
lah FYEH-stah

mistletoe
el muérdago
ehl MWEHR-dah-goh

fireworks
los fuegos artificiales
lohs FWEH-gohs ahr-tee-fee-THYAH-l

birthday
el cumpleaños
ehl koom-pleh-AH-nyohs

ceremony
la ceremonia
lah theh-reh-MOH-nyah

wedding ring
el anillo de bodas
ehl ah-NEE-yoh deh BOH-thahs

decorated eggs
huevos decorados
ohs WEH-bohs deh-koh-RAH-thoh

Easter Bunny
el Conejo de Pascua
ehl koh-NEH-khoh deh PAHS-kwah

New Year	**el Año Nuevo!**	ehl AH-nyoh NWEH-boh	All the best!	**¡Felicidades!**	feh-lee-thee-THAH-thehs!
Happy New Year!	**¡Feliz Año Nuevo!**	feh-LEETH AH-nyoh NWEH-boh!	Congratulations!	**¡Enhorabuena!**	ehn-oh-rah-BWEH-nah!
			Good luck!	**¡Buena suerte!**	BWEH-nah SWEHR-teh!
Happy Birthday!	**¡Feliz Cumpleaños!**	feh-LEETH koom-pleh-AH-nee-ohs	Merry Christmas!	**¡Feliz Navidad!**	feh-LEETH nah-bee-THATH!
			Happy Easter!	**¡Felices Pascuas!**	feh-LEE-thehs PAHS-kwahs!

Christianity
cristianismo
krees-tyah-NEES-moh

Confucianism
confucianismo
kohn-foo-thyah-NEES-moh

Jainism
jainismo
khah-ee-NEES-moh

Islam
islam
ees-LAHM

Buddhism
budismo
boo-DEES-moh

Judaism
judaísmo
khoo-thah-EES-moh

Hinduism
hinduismo
een-doo-EES-moh

Taoism
taoísmo
tah-oh-EES-moh

Sikhism
sijismo
see-KHEES-moh

to confess	**confesar**	kohn-feh-SAHR
without religious confession	**sin confesión religiosa**	seen kohn-feh-SYOHN reh-lee-KHYOH-sah
to believe in God	**creer en Dios**	kreh-EHR ehn DYOHS
to have faith	**tener fe**	teh-NEHR feh
to pray	**rezar**	rreh-THAHR

 HOME & HOUSEKEEPING

house
la casa
la KAH-sah

flat
el apartamento
ehl ah-pahr-tah-MEHN-toh

block of flats
el complejo residencial
ehl kohm-PLEH-khoh rreh-see-thehn-THYAL

duplex / two-storey house
el dúplex
el DOO-plex

detached house
la casa independiente
lah KAH-sah een-deh-pehn-DYEHN-teh

co-ownership
la copropiedad
lah KOH-proh-pyeh-THATH

houseboat
la casa flotante
lah KAH-sah floh-TAHN-teh

caravan
caravana
lah kah-rah-BAH-nah

farm
la granja
lah GRAHN-khah

flatshare
el apartamento compartido
ehl ah-pahr-tah-MEHN-toh kohm-pahr-TEE-thoh

Where do you live?	¿Dónde vives?	DOHN-deh BEE-behs?
I live in a flatshare.	Vivo en un apartamento compartido.	BEE-boh ehn oon ah-pahr-tah-MEHN-toh kohm-pahr-TEE-thoh
I live with my parents.	Vivo con mis padres.	BEE-boh kohn mees PAH-drehs

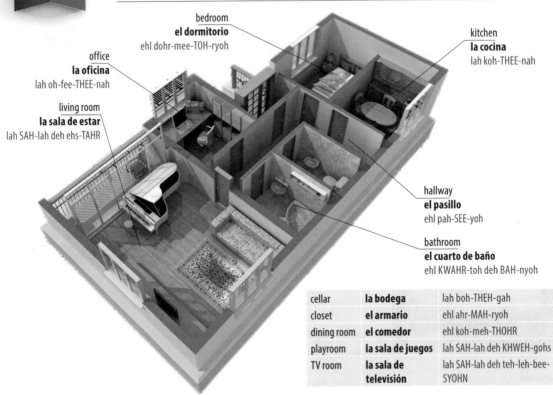

bedroom
el dormitorio
ehl dohr-mee-TOH-ryoh

kitchen
la cocina
lah koh-THEE-nah

office
la oficina
lah oh-fee-THEE-nah

living room
la sala de estar
lah SAH-lah deh ehs-TAHR

hallway
el pasillo
ehl pah-SEE-yoh

bathroom
el cuarto de baño
ehl KWAHR-toh deh BAH-nyoh

cellar	la bodega	lah boh-THEH-gah
closet	el armario	ehl ahr-MAH-ryoh
dining room	el comedor	ehl koh-meh-THOHR
playroom	la sala de juegos	lah SAH-lah deh KHWEH-gohs
TV room	la sala de televisión	lah SAH-lah deh teh-leh-bee-SYOHN

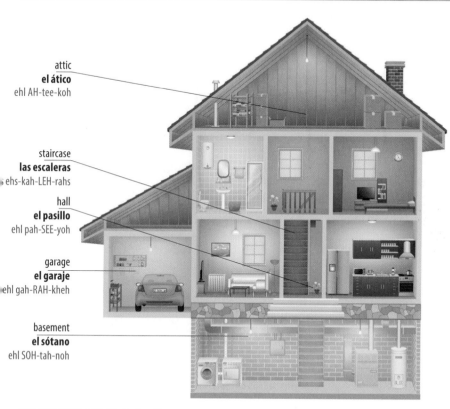

attic
el ático
ehl AH-tee-koh

staircase
las escaleras
ehs-kah-LEH-rahs

hall
el pasillo
ehl pah-SEE-yoh

garage
el garaje
ehl gah-RAH-kheh

basement
el sótano
ehl SOH-tah-noh

porch
el porche
ehl POHR-cheh

patio
el patio
ehl PAH-thyoh

workshop
el taller
ehl tah-YEHR

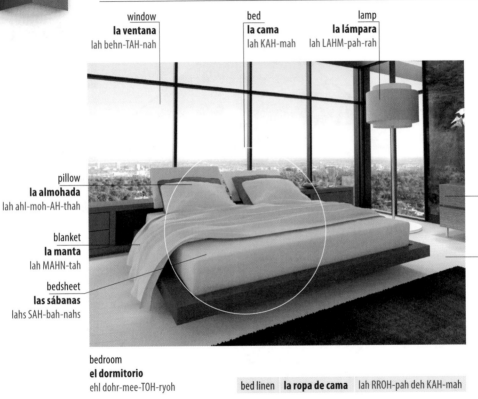

window
la ventana
lah behn-TAH-nah

bed
la cama
lah KAH-mah

lamp
la lámpara
lah LAHM-pah-rah

pillow
la almohada
lah ahl-moh-AH-thah

chest of drawers
la cómoda
lah KOH-moh-thah

blanket
la manta
lah MAHN-tah

carpet
la alfombra
lah ahl-FOHM-brah

bedsheet
las sábanas
lahs SAH-bah-nahs

bedroom
el dormitorio
ehl dohr-mee-TOH-ryoh

bed linen   **la ropa de cama**   lah RROH-pah deh KAH-mah

toilet
el inodoro
ehl ee-noh-THOH-roh

bidet
el bidé
ehl bee-THEH

mirror
el espejo
ehl ehs-PEH-khoh

shower
la ducha
lah DOO-chah

tap
el grifo
ehl GREE-foh

bath towel
la toalla
lah toh-AH-yah

wash basin
el lavado
ehl lah-BAH-thoh

flush
la cadena
lah kah-THEH-nah

bath **el baño** ehl BAH-nyoh

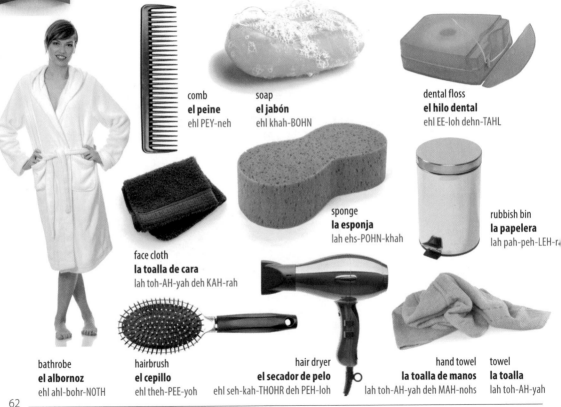

comb
el peine
ehl PEY-neh

soap
el jabón
ehl khah-BOHN

dental floss
el hilo dental
ehl EE-loh dehn-TAHL

sponge
la esponja
lah ehs-POHN-khah

rubbish bin
la papelera
lah pah-peh-LEH-r

face cloth
la toalla de cara
lah toh-AH-yah deh KAH-rah

bathrobe
el albornoz
ehl ahl-bohr-NOTH

hairbrush
el cepillo
ehl theh-PEE-yoh

hair dryer
el secador de pelo
ehl seh-kah-THOHR deh PEH-loh

hand towel
la toalla de manos
lah toh-AH-yah deh MAH-nohs

towel
la toalla
lah toh-AH-yah

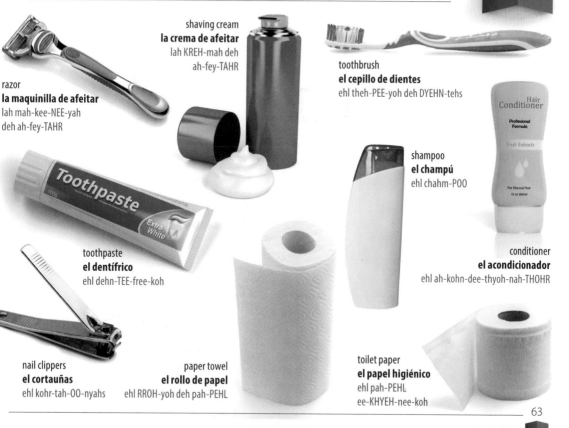

shaving cream
la crema de afeitar
lah KREH-mah deh
ah-fey-TAHR

toothbrush
el cepillo de dientes
ehl theh-PEE-yoh deh DYEHN-tehs

razor
la maquinilla de afeitar
lah mah-kee-NEE-yah
deh ah-fey-TAHR

shampoo
el champú
ehl chahm-POO

toothpaste
el dentífrico
ehl dehn-TEE-free-koh

conditioner
el acondicionador
ehl ah-kohn-dee-thyoh-nah-THOHR

nail clippers
el cortauñas
ehl kohr-tah-OO-nyahs

paper towel
el rollo de papel
ehl RROH-yoh deh pah-PEHL

toilet paper
el papel higiénico
ehl pah-PEHL
ee-KHYEH-nee-koh

63

fridge
la nevera
lah neh-BEH-rah

microwave
el microondas
ehl mee-kroh-OHN-dahs

stove
la estufa
lah ehs-TOO-fah

coffee machine
la máquina de café
lah MAH-kee-nah deh
kah-FEH

dishwasher
el lavavajillas
ehl lah-bah-bah-KHEE-yahs

freezer
el congelador
ehl kohn-kheh-lah-THOHR

washing machine
la lavadora
lah lah-bah-THOH-rah

oven
el horno
ehl OHR-noh

kettle
la tetera
lah teh-TEH-rah

toaster
la tostadora
lah tohs-tah-THOH-rah

cookery book
el libro de cocina
ehl LEE-broh deh koh-THEE-nah

dishcloth
el paño de cocina
ehl PAH-nyoh deh koh-THEE-nah

draining board
el escurridor
ehl ehs-koo-rree-THOHR

kitchen roll
el papel de cocina
ehl pah-PEHL deh koh-THEE-nah

plug
el tapón
ehl tah-POHN

tea towel
el paño de cocina
ehl PAH-nyoh deh koh-THEE-nah

shelf
el estante
ehl ehs-TAHN-teh

sink
el fregadero
ehl freh-gah-THEH-roh

tablecloth
el mantel
ehl mahn-TEHL

65

bottle opener
el abrebotellas
ehl ah-breh-boh-TEH-yahs

chopping board
la tabla de cortar
lah TAH-blah deh kohr-TAHR

colander
el colador
ehl koh-lah-THOHR

frying pan
la sartén
lah sahr-TEHN

grater
el rallador
ehl rrah-yah-THOHR

juicer
el exprimidor
ehl ehx-pree-mee-THOHR

corkscrew
el sacacorchos
ehl sah-kah-KOHR-chohs

kitchen scales
el peso de cocina
ehl PEH-soh deh koh-THEE-nah

mixing bowl
el cuenco
ehl KWEHN-ko

sieve
el colador
ehl koh-lah-THOHR

saucepan
la olla
lah OH-yah

whisk
la batidora
lah bah-tee-THOH-rah

tin opener
el abrelatas
ehl ah-breh-LAH-tahs

washing-up liquid
el lavavajillas
ehl lah-bah-bah-KHEE-yahs

to do the dishes / to do the washing up	**fregar los platos**	freh-GAHR los PLAH-tohs
to do the washing	**poner la lavadora**	poh-NEHR lah lah-bah-THOH-rah
to clear the table	**limpiar la mesa**	leem-PYAHR lah MEH-sah
to set the table	**poner la mesa**	poh-NEHR lah MEH-sah

cutlery	**los cubiertos**	lohs koo-BYEHR-tohs
dessert spoon	**la cuchara de postre**	lah koo-CHAH-rah deh POHS-treh
soup spoon	**la cuchara sopera**	lah koo-CHAH-rah soh-PEH-rah
spoon	**la cuchara**	lah koo-CHAH-rah

tablespoon
la cuchara
lah koo-CHAH-rah

fork
el tenedor
el teh-neh-THOHR

knife
el cuchillo
ehl koo-CHEE-yoh

teaspoon
la cucharilla
lah koo-chah-REE-yah

coffee spoon
la cucharilla de café
lah koo-chah-REE-yah
deh kah-FEH

plate
el plato
ehl PLAH-toh

mug
la taza
lah TAH-thah

sugar dispenser
el azucarero
ehl ah-thoo-kah-reh-roh

jug
la jarra
lah KHAHR-rah

saucer
el platillo
ehl plah-TEE-yoh

cup
la taza
lah TAH-thah

wine glass
la copa de vino
lah KOH-pah deh BEE-noh

teapot
la tetera
lah teh-TEH-rah

bowl
el cuenco
ehl KWEHN-koh

jar
el frasco
ehl FRAHS-koh

| crockery | **la vajilla** | lah bah-KHEE-yah |
| glass | **el vaso** | ehl BAH-soh |

armchair
el sillón
ehl see-YOHN

sofa
el sofá
ehl soh-FAH

lampshade
la pantalla
lah pahn-TAH-yah

lamp
la lámpara
lah LAHM-pah-rah

vase
el jarrón
ehl khah-RROHN

rug
la alfombra
lah ahl-FOHM-brah

bookcase
la estantería
lah ehs-tahn-teh-REE-yah

picture
el cuadro
ehl KWAH-droh

shelf
el estante
ehl ehs-TAHN-teh

table
la mesa
lah MEH-sah

plant
la planta
lah PLAHN-tah

chair
la silla
lah SEE-yah

I can relax here.	**Me puedo relajar aquí.**	meh PWEH-thoh rreh-lah-KHAR ah-KEE.
Do you watch TV often?	**¿Ves la televisión a menudo?**	behs lah teh-leh-bee-SYOHN ah meh-NOO-thoh?
What is the size of the living room?	**¿Cuál es el tamaño de la sala de estar?**	KWAHL ehs ehl tah-MAH-nyoh deh lah SAH-lah deh ehs-TAHR?

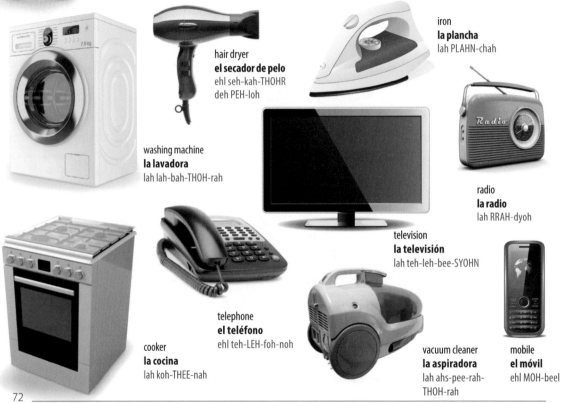

hair dryer
el secador de pelo
ehl seh-kah-THOHR
deh PEH-loh

iron
la plancha
lah PLAHN-chah

washing machine
la lavadora
lah lah-bah-THOH-rah

radio
la radio
lah RRAH-dyoh

television
la televisión
lah teh-leh-bee-SYOHN

telephone
el teléfono
ehl teh-LEH-foh-noh

cooker
la cocina
lah koh-THEE-nah

vacuum cleaner
la aspiradora
lah ahs-pee-rah-THOH-rah

mobile
el móvil
ehl MOH-beel

microwave
el microondas
ehl mee-kroh-OHN-dahs

coffee grinder
el molinillo de café
ehl moh-lee-NEE-yoh deh
kah-FEH

sewing machine
la máquina de coser
lah MAH-kee-nah deh
koh-SEHR

kettle
la tetera
lah teh-TEH-rah

refrigerator
la nevera
lah neh-BEH-rah

razor
**la maquinilla
de afeitar**
lah mah-kee-NEE-
yah deh ah-fey-TAHR

blender
la batidora
lah bah-tee-THOH-rah

mixer
la batidora
lah bah-tee-THOH-rah

gas stove
el hornillo a gas
ehl ohr-NEE-yoh ah GAHS

juicer
el exprimidor
ehl ehx-pree-mee-THOHR

to clean up
limpiar
leem-PYAHR

to dust
espolvorear
ehs-pohl-boh-reh-AHR

to vacuum
pasar la aspiradora
pah-SAHR lah ahs-pee-rah-THOH-rah

to clean the windows
limpiar las ventanas
leem-PYAHR lahs behn-TAH-nahs

to clean the floor
fregar el suelo
freh-GAHR ehl SWEH-loh

to do the washing/laundry
lavar la ropa
lah-BAHR lah RROH-pah

to do the dishes
fregar los platos
freh-GAHR lohs PLAH-tohs

to make the bed
hacer la cama
ah-THEHR lah KAH-mah

to hang up the laundry
colgar la ropa
kohl-GAHR lah RROH-pah

to iron
planchar
plahn-CHAHR

bucket
el cubo
ehl KOO-boh

dust cloth
el trapo
ehl TRAH-poh

feather duster
el plumero
ehl ploo-MEH-roh

mop
la fregona
lah freh-GOH-nah

broom
la escoba
lah ehs-KOH-bah

dustpan
el recogedor
ehl rreh-koh-kheh-THOHR

clothes line
el tendedero
ehl tehn-deh-THEH-roh

peg
las pinzas de la ropa
lahs PEEN-thahs deh lah RROH-pah

paper towel
el rollo de papel
ehl RROH-yoh deh pah-PEHL

laundry basket
el cesto de la ropa
ehl THES-toh deh lah RROH-pah

scrubbing brush
el cepillo
ehl theh-PEE-yoh

window cleaner
el limpiador de ventanas
ehl leem-pyah-THOHR deh behn-TAH-nahs

sponge
el estropajo
ehl ehs-troh-PAH-khoh

detergent
el detergente
ehl deh-tehr-KHEN-teh

We have to clean up.	**Tenemos que limpiar.**	teh-NEH-mohs keh leem-PYAHR
The flat is already clean.	**El apartamento ya está limpio.**	ehl ah-pahr-tah-MEHN-toh yah ehs-TAH LEEM-pyoh
Who does the cleaning?	**¿Quién hace la limpieza?**	KYEHN AH-theh lah leem-PYEH-thah?

 SCHOOL

white board
la pizarra
lah pee-THAH-rrah

chair
la silla
lah SEE-yah

book
el libro
ehl LEE-broh

table
la mesa
lah MEH-sah

clock
el reloj
ehl rreh-LOKH

teacher
el maestro *m* /
la maestra *f*
ehl mah-EH-stroh /
lah mah-EH-strah

student
el/la estudiante *m/f*
ehl/lah ehs-too-DYAHN-teh

tablet
la tableta / la tablet
lah tah-BLEH-tah /
lah TAH-bleht

calculator
la calculadora
lah kahl-koo-lah-THOH-rah

to go to school	**ir a la escuela**	eer ah lah ehs-KWEH-lah		marks	**las notas**	lahs NOH-tahs
to study	**estudiar**	ehs-too-DYAHR		an oral exam	**un examen oral**	oon ehx-AH-mehn oh-RAHL
to learn	**aprender**	ah-prehn-DEHR		a written exam	**un examen escrito**	oon ehx-AH-mehn ehs-KREE-toh
to do homework	**hacer la tarea**	ah-THEHR lohs deh-BEH-rehs		to prepare for an exam	**prepararse para un examen**	preh-pah-RAHR-seh PAH-rah oon ehx-AH-mehn
to know	**saber/conocer**	sah-BEHR / koh-noh-THEHR				
to take an exam	**hacer un examen**	ah-THEHR oon ehx-AH-mehn		to repeat a year	**repetir un año**	rreh-peh-TEER oon AH-nyoh
to pass	**aprobar**	ah-proh-BAHR				

Languages
los idiomas
lohs ee-DYOH-mahs

Spanish
español
ehs-pah-NYOHL

English
inglés
een-GLEHS

German
alemán
ah-leh-MAHN

French
francés
frahn-THEHS

Art
el arte
ehl AHR-teh

Geography
la geografía
lah kheh-oh-grah-FEE-yah

Music
la música
lah MOO-see-kah

History
la historia
lah ees-TOH-ryah

Chemistry
la química
lah KEE-mee-kah

Biology
la biología
lah byoh-loh-KHEE-yah

Mathematics
la matemática
lah mah-teh-MAH-tee-kah

Physical education
la educación física
lah eh-doo-kah-THYOHN
FEE-see-kah

scissors
las tijeras
lahs tee-KHEH-rahs

globe
el globo terráqueo
ehl GLOH-boh
teh-RRAH-keh-oh

school bag
la mochila
lah moh-CHEE-lah

pen
el bolígrafo
ehl boh-LEE-grah-foh

notebook
el cuaderno
ehl kwah-THEHR-noh

pencil case
el estuche
el ehs-TOO-cheh

ruler
la regla
lah RREH-glah

pencil
el lápiz
ehl LAH-peeth

pencil sharpener
el sacapuntas
ehl sah-kah-POON-tahs

rubber
la goma
lah GOH-mah

highlighter
el rotulador
ehl roh-too-lah-THOHR

book
el libro
ehl LEE-broh

colouring pen
el rotulador
ehl rroh-too-lah-THOHR

stapler
la grapadora
lah grah-pah-THOH-rah

 WORK

job interview
la entrevista de trabajo
lah ehn-treh-BEES-tah deh trah-BAH-khoh

recruiter
**el técnico
de selección
de personal**
ehl TEHK-nee-koh
deh seh-lehk-THYOHN
deh pehr-soh-NAHL

candidate
el candidato m / la candidata f
ehl kahn-dee-THAH-toh /
lah kahn-dee-THAH-tah

application letter
la carta de presentación
lah KAHR-tah deh
preh-sehn-tah-THYOHN

CV
el currículum vitae
ehl koo-RREE-koo-loom
BEE-teh

gross	**bruto**	BROO-toh
net	**neto**	NEH-toh
job advertisement	**la oferta de empleo / trabajo**	lah oh-FEHR-tah deh ehm-PLEH-oh / trah-BAH-khoh
application	**la carta de presentación**	lah KAHR-tah deh preh-sehn-tah-THYOHN
company	**la empresa**	lah ehm-PREH-sah
education	**la formación**	lah fohr-mah-THYOHN

interview	**la entrevista**	lah ehn-treh-BEES-tah
job	**el trabajo**	ehl trah-BAH-khoh
salary	**el salario**	ehl sah-LAH-ryoh
vacancy	**la vacante**	lah bah-KAHN-teh
work	**el trabajo**	ehl trah-BAH-khoh
to hire	**contratar**	kohn-trah-TAHR

experience	la experiencia	lah ehx-peh-RYEHN-thyah
to apply for	solicitar	soh-lee-thee-TAHR
assessment	la evaluación	lah eh-bah-loo-ah-THYOHN
bonus	el bonus	ehl BOH-noos
employer	el empleadro m / la empleadora f	ehl ehm-pleh-AH-THOR / lah ehm-pleh-oh-THOH-rah
to fire	despedir	dehs-peh-THEER
fringe benefits	las prestaciones complementarias	lahs preh-stah-THYOH-nehs kohm-pleh-mehn-TAH-ryahs
maternity leave	la baja por maternidad	lah BAH-khah pohr mah-tehr-nee-THATH
notice	la notificación	lah noh-tee-fee-kah-THYOHN
staff	el personal	ehl pehr-soh-NAHL
human resources officer	el encargado de personal	ehl ehn-kahr-GAH-thoh deh pehr-soh-NAHL
promotion	la promoción	lah proh-moh-THYOHN
prospects	las probabilidades	lahs proh-bah-bee-lee-THAH-thehs
to resign	renunciar	rreh-noon-THYAHR
to retire	jubilarse	khoo-bee-LAHR-seh
sick leave	la baja por enfermedad	lah BAH-khah pohr ehn-fehr-meh-THATH
strike	la huelga	lah WEL-gah
trainee	el becario m / la becaria f	ehl beh-KAH-ryoh / lah beh-KAH-ryah
training course	el curso de formación	ehl KOOR-soh deh fohr-mah-THYOHN
unemployment benefits	el subsidio por desempleo	ehl soob-SEE-thyoh pohr deh-sehm-PLEH-oh
workplace	el lugar de trabajo	ehl loo-GAHR deh trah-BAH-khoh

employee
el empleado m / la empleada f
ehl ehm-pleh-AH-thoh / lah ehm-pleh-AH-thah

actor
el actor *m* /
la actriz *f*
ehl ahk-TOHR /
lah ahk-TREETH

baker
el panadero *m* /
la panadera *f*
ehl pah-nah-THEH-roh /
lah pah-nah-THEH-rah

banker
el banquero *m* /
la banquera *f*
ehl bahn-KEH-roh /
lah bahn-KEH-rah

butcher
el carnicero *m* /
la carnicera *f*
ehl kahr-nee-THEH-roh
lah kahr-nee-THEH-rah

carpenter
el carpintero *m* /
la carpintera *f*
ehl kahr-peen-THEH-roh /
lah kahr-peen-THEH-rah

chef
el cocinero *m* /
la cocinera *f*
ehl koh-thee-NEH-roh /
lah koh-thee-NEH-rah

doctor
el médico *m* /
la médica *f*
ehl MEH-dee-koh /
lah MEH-dee-kah

farmer
el granjero *m* /
la granjera *f*
ehl grahn-KHEH-roh /
lah grahn-KHEH-rah

fisherman
el pescador *m* /
la pescadora *f*
ehl peh-skah-THOHR /
lah peh-skah-THOH-rah

firefighter
el bombero *m* /
la bombera *f*
ehl bohm-BEH-roh /
lah bohm-BEH-rah

musician
el músico *m* /
la música *f*
ehl MOO-see-koh /
lah MOO-see-kah

lawyer
el abogado *m* /
la abogada *f*
ehl ah-boh-GAH-thoh / lah ah-boh-GAH-thah

nurse
el enfermero *m* / la enfermera *f*
ehl ehn-fehr-MEH-roh /
lah ehn-fehr-MEH-rah

pilot
el piloto *m* / la piloto *f*
ehl pee-LOH-toh /
lah pee-LOH-toh

policeman
el policía *m* / la policía *f*
ehl poh-lee-THEE-yah /
lah poh-lee-THEE-yah

coach
el entrenador *m* / la entrenadora *f*
ehl ehn-treh-nah-THOHR /
lah ehn-treh-nah-THOH-rah

sailor
el marinero *m* / la marinera *f*
ehl mah-ree-NEH-roh /
lah mah-ree-NEH-rah

soldier
el soldado *m* / la soldado *f*
ehl sohl-DAH-thoh /
lah sohl-DAH-thoh

teacher
el maestro *m* / la maestra *f*
ehl mah-EHS-troh / lah
mah-EHS-trah

judge
el juez *m* / la juez *f*
ehl khweth /
lah khweth

tailor
el sastre *m* / la sastra *f*
ehl SAHS-treh /
lah SAHS-trah

veterinarian
el veterinario *m* / la veterinaria *f*
ehl beh-teh-ree-NAH-ryoh /
lah beh-teh-ree-NAH-ryah

waiter
el camarero *m* / la camarera *f*
ehl kah-mah-REH-roh /
lah kah-mah-REH-rah

mechanic
el mecánico *m* / la mecánica *f*
ehl meh-KAH-nee-koh /
lah meh-KAH-nee-kah

accountant	**el contable** *m* / **la contable** *f*	ehl kohn-TAH-bleh / lah kohn-TAH-bleh
barber	**el barbero** *m* / **la barbera** *f*	ehl bahr-BEH-roh / lah bahr-BEH-rah
beautician	**el esteticista** *m* / **la esteticista** *f*	ehl ehs-teh-tee-THEE-stah / lah ehs-teh-tee-THEE-stah
broker	**el corredor de bolsa** *m* / **la corredora de bolsa** *f*	ehl koh-rreh-THOHR deh BOHL-sah / lah koh-rreh-THOH-rah deh BOHL-sah
driver	**el chófer** *m* / **la chófer** *f*	ehl CHOH-fehr / lah CHOH-fehr
craftsman	**el artesano** *m* / **la artesana** *f*	ehl ahr-teh-SAH-noh / lah ahr-teh-SAH-nah
dentist	**el dentista** *m* / **la dentista** *f*	ehl dehn-TEE-stah / lah dehn-TEE-stah
engineer	**el ingeniero** *m* / **la ingeniera** *f*	ehl een-kheh-NYEH-roh / lah een-kheh-NYEH-rah
pharmacist	**el farmacéutico** *m* / **la farmacéutica** *f*	ehl fahr-mah-THEW-tee-koh / lah fahr-mah-THEW-tee-kah
writer	**el escritor** *m* / **la escritora** *f*	ehl ehs-kree-TOHR / lah ehs-kree-TOH-rah
politician	**el político** *m* / **la político** *f*	ehl poh-LEE-thee-koh / lah poh-LEE-thee-koh
professor	**el profesor** *m* / **la profesora** *f*	ehl proh-feh-SOHR / lah proh-feh-SOH-rah
salesman	**el vendedor** *m* / **la vendedora** *f*	ehl behn-deh-THOHR / lah behn-deh-THOH-rah
shoemaker	**el zapatero** *m* / **la zapatera** *f*	ehl thah-pah-TEH-roh / lah thah-pah-TEH-rah
watchmaker	**el relojero** *m* / **la relojera** *f*	ehl rreh-loh-KHEH-roh / lah rreh-loh-KHEH-rah
What's your occupation?	**¿Cuál es tu profesión?**	KWAL ehs too proh-feh-SYOHN?
I work as a secretary.	**Trabajo como secretaria.**	trah-BAH-khoh KOH-moh seh-kreh-TAH-ryah
I am a teacher.	**Soy maestra de profesión.**	Soy mah-EHS-trah deh proh-feh-SYOHN

desk
el escritorio
ehl ehs-kree-TOH-ryoh

office
la oficina
lah oh-fee-THEE-nah

computer
el ordenador
ehl ohr-deh-nah-THOHR

drawer
el cajón
ehl kah-KHOHN

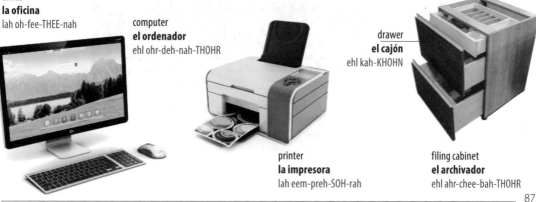

printer
la impresora
lah eem-preh-SOH-rah

filing cabinet
el archivador
ehl ahr-chee-bah-THOHR

rubber stamp
el sello
ehl SEH-yoh

telephone
el teléfono
ehl teh-LEH-foh-noh

ink pad
el tampón de tinta
ehl tahm-POHN deh TEEN-tah

bin
la papelera
lah pah-peh-LEH-rah

keyboard
el teclado
ehl teh-KLAH-thoh

swivel chair
la silla giratoria
lah SEE-yah khee-rah-TOH-ryah

clipboard	**el portapapeles**	ehl pohr-tah-pah-PEH-lehs
file	**el archivo**	ehl ahr-CHEE-boh
in-tray	**la bandeja de entrada**	lah bahn-DEH-khah deh ehn-TRAH-thah
to photocopy	**fotocopiar**	foh-toh-koh-PYAHR
to print	**imprimir**	eem-pree-MEER

bulldog clip
el clip
ehl kleep

calculator
la calculadora
lah kahl-koo-lah-THOH-rah

correction tape
el típex
ehl TEE-pex

laptop
el portátil
ehl pohr-TAH-teel

highlighter
el rotulador
ehl roh-too-lah-THOHR

envelope
el sobre
ehl SOH-breh

letterhead
el membrete
ehl mehm-BREH-teh

holepunch
la perforadora
lah pehr-foh-rah-THOH-rah

elastic bands
las bandas elásticas
lahs BAHN-dahs eh-LAHS-tee-kahs

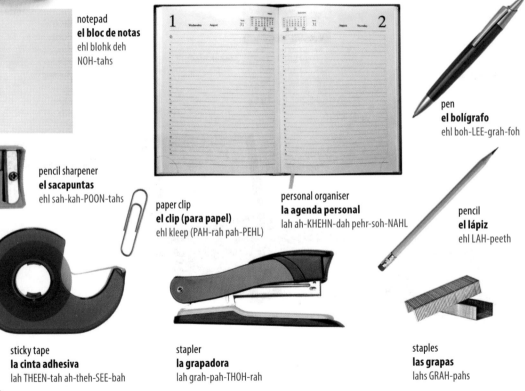

notepad
el bloc de notas
ehl blohk deh
NOH-tahs

pencil sharpener
el sacapuntas
ehl sah-kah-POON-tahs

paper clip
el clip (para papel)
ehl kleep (PAH-rah pah-PEHL)

personal organiser
la agenda personal
lah ah-KHEHN-dah pehr-soh-NAHL

pen
el bolígrafo
ehl boh-LEE-grah-foh

pencil
el lápiz
ehl LAH-peeth

sticky tape
la cinta adhesiva
lah THEEN-tah ah-theh-SEE-bah

stapler
la grapadora
lah grah-pah-THOH-rah

staples
las grapas
lahs GRAH-pahs

FOOD AND DRINK

apple juice
el zumo de manzana
ehl THOO-moh deh
mahn-THAH-nah

grapefruit juice
el zumo de pomelo
ehl THOO-moh deh
poh-MEH-loh

orange juice
**el zumo de
naranja**
ehl THOO-moh deh
nah-RAHN-khah

tomato juice
el zumo de tomate
ehl THOO-moh deh toh-
MAH-teh

coffee
el café
ehl kah-FEH

milk
la leche
lah LEH-cheh

tea
el té
ehl teh

with lemon
con limón
kohn lee-MOHN

water
el agua
ehl AHK-wah

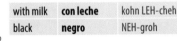

| with milk | **con leche** | kohn LEH-cheh | decaffeinated | **descafeinado** | dehs-kah-feh-ee-NAH-thoh |
| black | **negro** | NEH-groh | fruit juice | **el zumo de frutas** | ehl THOO-moh deh FROO-tahs |

bacon
el beicon
ehl BEY-kohn

banana
el plátano
ehl PLAH-tah-noh

berries
las bayas
lahs BAH-yahs

biscuit
la galleta
lah gah-YEH-tah

blueberries
los arándanos
lohs ah-RAHN-dah-nohs

bread
el pan
ehl pahn

jam
la mermelada
lah mehr-meh-LAH-thah

butter
la mantequilla
lah mahn-teh-KEE-yah

cereal
los cereales
lohs theh-reh-AH-lehs

cheese
el queso
ehl KEH-soh

cottage cheese
el requesón
ehl rreh-keh-SOHN

doughnut
el dónut
ehl DOH-noot

93

egg
el huevo
ehl WEH-boh

ham
el jamón
ehl khah-MOHN

honey
la miel
lah myehl

marmalade
la mermelada
lah mehr-meh-LAH-tha

omelette
la tortilla
lah tohr-TEE-ya

pancake
la crepe / crep
lah KREH-peh / krehp

peanut butter
la crema de cacahuetes
lah KREH-mah deh kah-kah-WEH-tehs

sandwich
el bocadillo
ehl boh-kah-DEE-yoh

sausage
la salchicha
lah sahl-CHEE-cha

toast
la tostada
lah tohs-TAH-thah

waffle
el gofre
ehl GOH-freh

yoghurt
el yogur
ehl yoh-GOOR

breakfast
el desayuno
ehl deh-sah-YOO-noh

brunch
el almuerzo
ehl ahl-MWER-thoh

porridge
las gachas
lahs GAH-chahs

scrambled eggs
los huevos revueltos
lohs WEH-bohs rreh-BWEHL-tohs

hard-boiled egg
el huevo duro
ehl WEH-boh DOO-roh

soft-boiled egg
el huevo pasado por agua
ehl WEH-boh pah-sah-THOH pohr AHK-wah

What do you eat for breakfast?	**¿Qué comes para desayunar?**	KEH KOH-mehs PAH-rah deh-sah-yoo-NAHR?
When do you have breakfast?	**¿Cuándo tienes el desayuno?**	KWAHN-doh TYEH-nehs ehl deh-sah-YOO-noh?
When does breakfast start?	**¿Cuándo comienza el desayuno?**	KWAHN-doh koh-MYEHN-thah ehl deh-sah-YOO-noh?
What would you like to drink?	**¿Qué te gustaría beber?**	keh teh goos-tah-REE-yah beh-BEHR?
I would like a white tea.	**Quisiera un té blanco por favor.**	kee-SYEH-rah oon teh BLAHN-koh pohr fah-BOHR

bacon
la panceta
lah pahn-THEH-tah

beef
la carne de vaca
lah KAHR-neh deh BAH-kah

chicken
el pollo
ehl POH-yoh

duck
el pato
ehl PAH-toh

ham
el jamón
ehl khah-MOHN

kidneys
los riñones
lohs ree-NYOH-nehs

lamb
el cordero
ehl kohr-DEH-roh

liver
el hígado
ehl EE-gah-thoh

mince
la carne picada
lah KAHR-neh pee-KAH-thah

pâté
el paté
ehl pah-TEH

salami
el salami
ehl sah-LAH-mee

meat
la carne
lah KAHR-neh

rabbit
el conejo
ehl koh-NEH-khoh

pork
la carne de cerdo
lah KAHR-neh deh THER-doh

sausage
la salchicha
lah sahl-CHEE-chah

turkey
el pavo
ehl PAH-boh

veal
la carne de ternera
lah KAHR-neh deh tehr-NEH-rah

97

fruits
la fruta
lah FROO-tah

apple
la manzana
lah mahn-THAH-nah

apricot
el albaricoque
ehl ahl-bah-ree-KOH-keh

banana
el plátano
ehl PLAH-tah-noh

blackberry
la mora
lah MOH-rah

blackcurrant
la grosella negra
lah groh-SEH-yah NEH-grah

blueberry
el arándano
ehl ah-RAHN-dah-noh

cherry
la cereza
lah theh-REH-thah

coconut
el coco
ehl KOH-koh

fig
el higo
ehl EE-goh

grape
la uva
lah OO-bah

grapefruit
el pomelo
ehl poh-MEH-loh

kiwi fruit
el kiwi
ehl KEE-wee

lemon
el limón
ehl lee-MOHN

lime
la lima
lah LEE-mah

mango
el mango
ehl MAHN-goh

melon
el melón
ehl meh-LOHN

orange
la naranja
lah nah-RAHN-khah

peach
el melocotón
ehl meh-loh-koh-TOHN

pear
la pera
lah PEH-rah

lychee
el lichi
ehl LEE-chee

clementine
la clementina
lah kleh-mehn-TEE-nah

papaya
la papaya
lah pah-PAH-yah

pineapple
la piña
lah PEE-nyah

watermelon
la sandía
lah sahn-DEE-yah

kumquat
el quinoto
ehl kee-NOH-toh

nectarine
la nectarina
lah nehk-tah-REE-nah

raspberry
la frambuesa
lah frahm-BWEH-sah

persimmon
el caqui
ehl KAH-kee

plum
la ciruela
lah thee-RWEH-lah

redcurrant
la grosella roja
lah groh-SEH-yah
RROH-khah

rhubarb
el ruibarbo
ehl rrwee-BAHR-boh

pomegranate
la granada
lah grah-NAH-thah

strawberry
la fresa
lah FREH-sah

passion fruit
la fruta de la pasión / la maracuyá
lah FROO-tah deh lah pah-SYOHN /
lah mah-rah-koo-YAH

vegetables
las verduras
lahs behr-DOO-rahs

artichoke
la alcachofa
lah ahl-kah-CHOH-fah

asparagus
los espárragos
lohs ehs-PAHR-rah-gohs

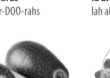

avocado
el aguacate
ehl ahk-wah-KAH-teh

beansprouts
los brotes de soja
lohs BROH-tehs deh SOH-khah

beetroot
la remolacha
lah rreh-moh-LAH-chah

broccoli
el brócoli
ehl BROH-koh-lee

Brussels sprouts
las coles de Bruselas
lahs KOH-lehs deh broo-SEH-lahs

cabbage
el repollo
ehl rreh-POH-yoh

aubergine
la berenjena
lah beh-rehn-KHEH-nah

carrot
la zanahoria
lah thah-nah-OH-ryah

101

cauliflower
la coliflor
lah koh-lee-FLOHR

celery
el apio
ehl AH-pyoh

courgette
el calabacín
ehl kah-lah-bah-THEEN

cucumber
el pepino
ehl peh-PEE-noh

garlic
el ajo
ehl AH-khoh

ginger
el jengibre
ehl khehn-KHEE-breh

leek
el puerro
ehl PWEH-rroh

lettuce
la lechuga
lah leh-CHOO-gah

mushroom
el champiñón
ehl cham-pee-NYOHN

onion
la cebolla
lah theh-BOH-yah

peas
los guisantes
lohs gea-SAHN-tehs

potato
la patata
lah pah-TAH-tah

spinach
la espinaca
lah ehs-pee-NAH-kah

radish
el rábano
ehl RRAH-bah-noh

pumpkin
la calabaza
lah kah-lah-BAH-thah

sweetcorn
el maíz
ehl mah-EETH

tomato
el tomate
ehl toh-MAH-teh

spring onion
la cebolleta
lah theh-boh-YEH-tah

red pepper
el pimiento rojo
ehl pee-MYEHN-toh RROH-khoh

green beans
las judías verdes
lahs khoo-THEE-yahs BEHR-dehs

chicory
la endibia
lah ehn-DEE-byah

turnip
el nabo
ehl NAH-boh

cuttlefish
la sepia
lah SEH-pyah

haddock
el eglefino
ehl eh-gleh-FEE-noh

lemon sole
el lenguado
ehl lehn-GWAH-thoh

halibut
el fletán
ehl fleh-TAHN

mackerel
la caballa
lah kah-BAH-yah

monkfish
el rape
ehl RRAH-peh

mussels
los mejillones
lohs meh-khee-YOH-nehs

sardine
la sardina
lah sahr-DEE-nah

sea bass
la lubina
lah loo-BEE-nah

sea bream
la dorada
lah doh-RAH-thah

swordfish
el pez espada
ehl peth ehs-PAH-thah

trout
la trucha
lah TROO-chah

crab
el cangrejo
ehl kahn-GREH-khoh

crayfish
el cangrejo de río
ehl kahn-GREH-khoh deh RREE-yoh

lobster
el bogavante
ehl boh-gah-BAHN-teh

tuna
el atún
ehl ah-TOON

octopus
el pulpo
ehl POOL-poh

oyster
la ostra
lah OHS-trah

prawn / shrimp
el camarón
ehl kah-mah-ROHN

scallop
la vieira
lah BYEY-rah

salmon
el salmón
ehl sahl-MOHN

squid
el calamar
ehl kah-lah-MAHR

fish	**el pescado**	ehl pehs-KAH-thoh
cleaned	**limpio**	LEEM-pyoh
fresh	**fresco**	FREHS-koh
frozen	**congelado**	kohn-kheh-LAH-thoh
salted	**salado**	sah-LAH-thoh
skinned	**pelado**	peh-LAH-thoh
smoked	**ahumado**	ah-oo-MAH-thoh

cheese
el queso
ehl KEH-soh

cream
la nata
lah NAH-tah

egg
el huevo
ehl WEH-boh

milk
la leche
la LEH-cheh

cottage cheese
el requesón
ehl rreh-keh-SOHN

blue cheese
el queso azul
ehl KEH-soh ah-THOOL

butter
la mantequilla
lah mahn-teh-KEE-yah

goat's cheese	**el queso de cabra**	ehl KEH-soh deh KAH-brah	skimmed milk	**la leche desnatada**	lah LEH-cheh dehs-nah-TAH-thah
margarine	**la margarina**	lah mahr-gha-REE-nah			
full-fat milk	**la leche entera**	lah LEH-cheh ehn-TEH-rah	sour cream	**la nata agria**	lah NAH-tah AH-gryah
semi-skimmed milk	**la leche semidesnatada**	lah LEH-cheh SEH-mee-dehs-nah-TAH-thah	yoghurt	**el yogur**	ehl yoh-GOOR
			crème fraîche	**la crema fresca**	lah KREH-mah FREHS-kah

baguette
la baguette
lah bah-GET

bread rolls
los panecillos
lohs pah-neh-THEE-yohs

brown bread
el pan integral
ehl pahn een-teh-GRAHL

cake
la torta
lah TOHR-tah

loaf
el pan
ehl pahn

white bread
el pan blanco
ehl pahn BLAHN-koh

garlic bread	**el pan de ajo**	ehl pahn deh AH-khoh	quiche	**el/la quiche**	ehl/lah KEE-cheh
pastry	**los pasteles**	lohs pahs-TEH-lehs	sliced loaf	**el pan de molde**	ehl pahn deh MOHL-deh
pitta bread	**el pan de pita**	ehl pahn deh PEE-tah	sponge cake	**el bizcocho**	ehl beeth-KOH-choh

ketchup
el kétchup
ehl KEH-choop

mayonnaise
la mayonesa
lah mah-yoh-NEH-sah

mustard
la mostaza
lah mohs-TAH-thah

vinegar
el vinagre
ehl bee-NAH-greh

salt
la sal
lah sahl

pepper
la pimienta
lah pee-MYEHN-ta

basil	**la albahaca**	lah ahl-bah-AH-kah	paprika	**el pimentón**	ehl pee-mehn-TOHN
chilli powder	**el polvo de chile**	ehl POHL-boh deh CHEE-leh	parsley	**el perejil**	ehl peh-reh-KHEEL
chives	**el cebollino**	ehl theh-boh-YEE-noh	rosemary	**el romero**	ehl rroh-MEH-roh
cinnamon	**la canela**	lah kah-NEH-lah	saffron	**el azafrán**	ehl ah-thah-FRAHN
coriander	**el cilantro**	ehl thee-LAHN-troh	sage	**la salvia**	lah SAHL-byah
cumin	**el comino**	ehl koh-MEE-noh	salad dressing	**la vinagreta**	lah bee-nah-GREH-tah
curry	**el curry**	ehl KOO-rree	spices	**las especias**	lahs ehs-PEH-thyahs
dill	**el eneldo**	ehl eh-NEHL-doh	thyme	**el tomillo**	ehl toh-MEE-yoh
nutmeg	**la nuez moscada**	lah nweth mohs-KAH-thah	vinaigrette	**la vinagreta**	lah bee-nah-GREH-tah

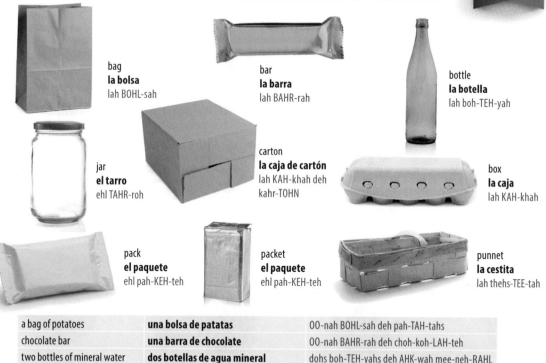

bag
la bolsa
lah BOHL-sah

bar
la barra
lah BAHR-rah

bottle
la botella
lah boh-TEH-yah

jar
el tarro
ehl TAHR-roh

carton
la caja de cartón
lah KAH-khah deh
kahr-TOHN

box
la caja
lah KAH-khah

pack
el paquete
ehl pah-KEH-teh

packet
el paquete
ehl pah-KEH-teh

punnet
la cestita
lah thehs-TEE-tah

a bag of potatoes	**una bolsa de patatas**	OO-nah BOHL-sah deh pah-TAH-tahs
chocolate bar	**una barra de chocolate**	OO-nah BAHR-rah deh choh-koh-LAH-teh
two bottles of mineral water	**dos botellas de agua mineral**	dohs boh-TEH-yahs deh AHK-wah mee-neh-RAHL
a carton of milk	**un tetrabrik de leche**	oon teh-trah-BREEK deh LEH-cheh
a jar of jam	**un tarro de mermelada**	oon TAHR-roh deh mehr-meh-LAH-thah

biscuit
la galleta
lah gah-YEH-tah

chocolate bar
la tableta de chocolate
lah tah-BLEH-tah deh choh-koh-LAH-teh

chocolate cake
el pastel de chocolate
ehl pahs-TEHL deh choh-koh-LAH-teh

apple pie
la tarta de manzana
lah TAHR-tah deh mahn-THAH-nah

doughnut
el dónut
ehl DOH-noot

fruit cake
el pastel de frutas
ehl pahs-TEHL deh FROO-tahs

fruit salad
la ensalada de frutas
lah ehn-sah-LAH-thah
deh FROO-tahs

cheesecake
la tarta de queso
lah TAHR-tah deh
KEH-soh

gingerbread
el pan de jengibre
ehl pahn deh khehn-KHEE-breh

ice cream
el helado
ehl eh-LAH-thoh

muffin
la magdalena
lah mah-thah-LEH-nah

chocolate mousse
la espuma de chocolate
lah ehs-POO-mah deh
choh-koh-LAH-teh

milkshake
el batido
ehl bah-TEE-thoh

marshmallow
la nube
lah NOO-beh

macaroon
el macarrón
ehl mah-kah-RROHN

waffle
el gofre
el GOH-freh

pancakes
las crepes/creps
lahs KREH-pehs/krehps

strudel
el pastel de hojaldre
ehl pahs-TEHL deh oh-KHAHL-dreh

pudding
el pudin
ehl POO-deen

honey
la miel
lah myehl

cake	**la tarta**	lah TAHR-tah
coconut cake	**la tarta de coco**	lah TAHR-tah deh KOH-koh
dessert	**el postre**	ehl POHS-treh
frozen yoghurt	**el yogur helado**	ehl yoh-GOOR eh-LAH-thoh
rice pudding	**el arroz con leche**	ehl ah-RROTH kohn LEH-cheh
I like to eat sweets.	**Me gusta comer dulces.**	meh GOOS-tah koh-MEHR DOOL-thehs
I cannot eat anything sweet.	**No puedo comer nada dulce.**	noh PWEH-thoh koh-MEHR NAH-thah DOOL-theh

cheeseburger
la hamburguesa de queso
lah ahm-boor-GEH-sah deh KEH-soh

hot dog
el perrito caliente
ehl peh-RREE-toh kah-LYEHN-teh

fish sandwich
el bocadillo con pescado
ehl boh-KAH-dee-yoh kohn
pehs-KAH-thoh

fried chicken
el pollo frito
ehl POH-yoh FREE-toh

French fries
las patatas fritas
lahs pah-TAH-tahs FREE-tahs

nachos
los nachos
lohs NAH-chohs

taco
el taco
ehl TAH-koh

burrito
el burrito
ehl boo-RREE-toh

pizza
la pizza
lah PEE-tsah

hamburger
la hamburguesa
lah ahm-boor-GEH-sah

chicken sandwich
el bocadillo de pollo
ehl boh-KAH-dee-yoh deh POH-yoh

fish and chips
pescado y patatas fritas
pehs-KAH-thoh ee pah-TAH-tahs
FREE-tahs

to peel	pelar	peh-LAHR
to grate	rallar	rrah-YAHR
to chop	picar	pee-KAHR
to crush	aplastar	ah-plahs-TAHR
to beat	morder	mohr-DEHR
to grease	engrasar	ehn-grah-SAHR
to break	romper	rrohm-PEHR
to stir	agitar	ah-khee-TAHR
to knead	amasar	ah-mah-SAHR
to steam	cocer al vapor	koh-THEHR ahl bah-POHR
to weigh	pesar	peh-SAHR
to add	añadir	ah-nyah-THEER
to bake	hornear	ohr-neh-AHR
to stir-fry	sofreír	soh-freh-EER
to grill	asar a la parrilla	ah-SAHR ah lah pah-RREE-yah
to roast	asar	ah-SAHR
to barbecue	hacer una barbacoa	ah-THEHR OO-nah bahr-bah-KOH-ah
to fry	freír	freh-EER

to.wash
lavar
lah-BAHR

to mix
mezclar
meth-KLAHR

to cut
cortar
kohr-TAHR

to boil
hervir
ehr-BEER

bar
el bar
ehl bahr

buffet
el bufé
ehl boo-FEH

bill
la cuenta
lah KWEHN-tah

bistro
el restaurante
ehl rehs-taw-RAHN-teh

café
la cafetería
lah kah-feh-teh-REE-yah

dessert
el postre
ehl POHS-treh

menu
la carta
lah KAHR-tah

canteen
la cantina
lah kahn-TEE-nah

pizzeria
la pizzería
lah pee-tseh-REE-yah

pub
el pub
ehl poob

salad bar
la barra de ensaladas
lah BAH-rrah deh ehn-sah-LAH-thahs

deli
el/la delicatessen
ehl/lah deh-lee-kah-TEH-ssehn

115

self-service
autoservicio
ahw-toh-sehr-BEE-thyoh

take-out / take-away
comida para llevar
lah koh-MEE-thah PAH-rah yeh-BAHR

waiter
el camarero
ehl kah-mah-REH-roh

waitress
la camarera
lah kah-mah-REH-rah

à la carte	**a la carta**	ah lah KAHR-tah
starter	**EL aperitivo**	ehl ah-peh-ree-TEE-boh
booking	**la reserva**	lah rreh-SEHR-bah
complimentary	**gratuito**	grah-TWEE-toh
dish	**el plato**	ehl PLAH-toh
main course	**el plato principal**	el PLAH-toh preen-thee-PAHL
to order	**pedir**	peh-THEER
speciality	**la especialidad**	lah ehs-peh-thyah-lee-THATH
aperitif	**el aperitivo**	el ah-peh-ree-TEE-voh

What do you want to order?	**¿Qué te gustaría pedir?**	KEH teh goo-stah-REE-yah peh-THEER?
I would like to see the menu.	**La carta por favor.**	lah KAHR-tah pohr fah-BOHR
We'll take the set menu.	**Tomaremos el menu del día.**	toh-mah-REH-mohs ehl meh-NOO dehl DEE-yah

 TRAVEL AND LEISURE

to travel by bus
viajar en autobús
byah-KHAHR ehn ahw-toh-BOOS

to travel by plane
viajar en avión
byah-KHAHR ehn ah-BYOHN

to travel by car
viajar en coche
byah-KHAHR ehn KOH-cheh

to travel by bicycle
viajar en bicicleta
byah-KHAHR ehn bee-thee-KLEH-ta

to travel by motorcycle
viajar en moto
byah-yah-KHAHR ehn MOH-toh

travel agency
la agencia de viajes
lah ah-KHEHN-thyah deh BYAH-khehs

family holiday
las vacaciones en familia
lahs bah-kah-THYOH-nehs ehn
fah-MEE-lyah

safari
el safari
ehl sah-FAH-ree

honeymoon
la luna de miel
lah LOO-nah deh myehl

beach holiday
las vacaciones en la playa
lahs bah-kah-THYOH-nehs ehn lah
PLAH-yah

round-the-world trip
el viaje alrededor del mundo
ehl BYAH-kheh ahl-reh-theh-
THOHR dehl MOON-doh

cruise
el crucero
ehl kroo-THEH-roh

to book
reservar
rreh-sehr-BAHR

long-haul destination
el destino de larga distancia
ehl dehs-TEE-noh deh LAHR-gah
dees-TAHN-

guided tour
la visita guiada
lah bee-SEE-tah gea-YAH-thah

out of season
fuera de temporada
FWEH-rah deh tehm-poh-
RAH-thah

picturesque village
el pueblo pintoresco
ehl PWEH-bloh peen-toh-REHS-koh

landscape
el paisaje
ehl pay-SAH-kheh

to go sightseeing
hacer turismo
ah-THEHR too-REES-moh

city break
la escapada a una ciudad
lah ehs-kah-PAH-thah ah
OO-nah thyoo-THATH

holiday brochure	**el folleto de vacaciones**	ehl foh-YEH-toh deh bah-kah-THYOH-nehs
holiday destination	**el destino**	ehl dehs-TEE-noh
package tour	**el paquete turístico**	ehl pah-KEH-teh too-REES-tee-koh
places of interest	**los lugares de interés**	lohs loo-GAH-rehs deh een-teh-REHS
short break	**la escapada**	lah ehs-kah-PAH-thah
tourist attractions	**las atracciones turísticas**	lahs ah-trahk-THYOH-nehs too-REES-tee-kahs
tourist trap	**la trampa para turistas**	lah TRAHM-pah PAH-rah too-REES-tahs

Afghanistan
Afganistán
ahf-gah-nees-TAHN

Angola
Angola
ahn-GOH-lah

Aruba
Aruba
ah-ROO-bah

The Bahamas
Las Bahamas
lahs bah-AH-mahs

Belarus
Bielorrusia
byeh-loh-RROO-syah

Albania
Albania
ahl-BAH-nyah

Antigua and Barbuda
Antigua y Barbuda
ahn-TEE-gwah y bahr-BOO-thah

Australia
Australia
ahws-TRAH-lyah

Bahrain
Bahréin
bah-REYHN

Belgium
Bélgica
BEHL-khee-kah

Algeria
Argelia
ahr-KHEH-lyah

Argentina
Argentina
ahr-khehn-TEE-nah

Austria
Austria
AHWS-tryah

Bangladesh
Bangladesh
bahn-glah-DEHS

Belize
Belice
beh-LEE-theh

Andorra
Andorra
ahn-DOH-rrah

Armenia
Armenia
ahr-MEH-nyah

Azerbaijan
Azerbaiyán
ah-thehr-ba-ee-YAHN

Barbados
Barbados
bahr-BAH-thohs

Benin
Benín
beh-NEEN

Bhutan
Bután
booh-TAHN

Brazil
Brasil
brah-SEEL

Burma
Birmania
beer-MAH-nyah

Canada
Canadá
kah-nah-THAH

Chile
Chile
CHEE-leh

Bolivia
Bolivia
boh-LEE-byah

Brunei
Brunéi
broo-NEH-ee

Burundi
Burundi
boo-ROON-dee

Cape Verde
Cabo Verde
KAH-boh BEHR-deh

China
China
CHEE-nah

Bosnia and Herzegovina
Bosnia y Herzegovina
BOHS-nyah ee ehr-tseh-
goh-BEE-nah

Bulgaria
Bulgaria
bool-GAH-ryah

Cambodia
Camboya
kahm-BOH-yah

Central African Republic
República Centroafricana
reh-POO-blee-kah THEHN-troh-
ah-free-KAH-nah

Colombia
Colombia
koh-LOHM-byah

Botswana
Botsuana
bohts-WAH-nah

Burkina Faso
Burkina Faso
boor-KEE-nah FAH-soh

Cameroon
Camerún
kah-meh-ROON

Chad
Chad
chahth

Comoros
Comoras
koh-MOH-rahs

Democratic Republic
of the Congo
**República Democrática
del Congo**
reh-POO-blee-kah deh-moh-
KRAH-tee-kah dehl KOHN-goh

Republic of the Congo
República del Congo
reh-POO-blee-kah
dehl KOHN-goh

Costa Rica
Costa Rica
KOHS-tah RREE-kah

Côte d'Ivoire
Costa de Marfil
KOHS-tah deh MAHR-feel

Croatia
Croacia
kroh-AH-thyah

Cuba
Cuba
KOO-bah

Curacao
Curazao
koo-rah-THAHW

Cyprus
Chipre
CHEE-preh

Czechia
República Checa
reh-POO-blee-kah CHEH-kah

Denmark
Dinamarca
dee-nah-MAHR-kah

Djibouti
Yibuti
yee-BOO-tee

Dominica
Dominica
doh-mee-NEE-kah

Dominican Republic
República Dominicana
reh-POO-blee-kah doh-mee-
neeh-KAH-nah

East Timor
Timor Oriental
tee-MOHR oh-ryehn-TAHL

Ecuador
Ecuador
eh-kwah-THOHR

Egypt
Egipto
eh-KHEEP-toh

El Salvador
El Salvador
ehl sahl-bah-THOHR

Equatorial Guinea
Guinea Ecuatorial
gea-NEH-ah eh-
kwah-toh-RYAHL

Eritrea
Eritrea
eh-ree-TREH-ah

Estonia
Estonia
ehs-TOH-nyah

France
Francia
FRAHN-thyah

Germany
Alemania
ah-leh-MAH-nyah

Guatemala
Guatemala
gwah-teh-MAH-lah

Haiti
Haití
ah-ee-TEEH

Ethiopia
Etiopía
eh-tyoh-PEE-yah

Gabon
Gabón
gah-BOHN

Ghana
Ghana
GAH-nah

Guinea
Guinea
gea-NEH-ah

Honduras
Honduras
ohn-DOO-rahs

Fiji
Fiyi
FEE-yee

The Gambia
Gambia
GAHM-byah

Greece
Grecia
GREH-thyah

Guinea-Bissau
Guinea-Bissau
gea-NEH-ah bee-SAHW

Hong Kong
Hong Kong
ohn-KOHN

Finland
Finlandia
feen-LAHN-dyah

Georgia
Georgia
kheh-OHR-khyah

Grenada
Granada
grah-NAH-thah

Guyana
Guayana
gwah-YAH-nah

Hungary
Hungría
oon-GREE-yah

Iceland
Islandia
ees-LAHN-dyah

Iraq
Irak
ee-RAHK

Jamaica
Jamaica
khah-MAY-kah

Kenya
Kenia
KEH-nyah

Kosovo
Kosovo
koh-SOH-boh

India
India
EEN-dyah

Ireland
Irlanda
eer-LAHN-dah

Japan
Japón
khah-POHN

Kiribati
Kiribati
kee-ree-BAH-tee

Kuwait
Kuwait
koo-BAYHT

Indonesia
Indonesia
een-doh-NEH-syah

Israel
Israel
ees-rah-EHL

Jordan
Jordania
khohr-DAH-nyah

North Korea
Corea del Norte
koh-REH-ah dehl NOHR-teh

Kyrgyzstan
Kirguistán
keer-geas-TAHN

Iran
Irán
ee-RAHN

Italy
Italia
ee-TAH-lyah

Kazakhstan
Kazajistán
kah-thah-khees-TAHN

South Korea
Corea del Sur
koh-REH-ah dehl SOOR

Laos
Laos
LAH-ohs

Latvia
Letonia
leh-TOH-nyah

Libya
Libia
LEE-byah

Macau
Macau
mah-KAHW

Malaysia
Malasia
mah-LAH-syah

Marshall Islands
Islas Marshall
EES-lahs MAHR-shahl

Lebanon
Líbano
LEE-bah-noh

Liechtenstein
Liechtenstein
LEEKH-tehn-steyn

Macedonia
Macedonia
mah-theh-THOH-nyah

Maldives
Maldivas
mahl-DEE-bahs

Mauritania
Mauritania
mahw-ree-TAH-nyah

Lesotho
Lesoto
leh-SOH-toh

Lithuania
Lituania
lee-too-AH-nyah

Madagascar
Madagascar
mah-thah-gahs-KAHR

Mali
Mali
MAH-lee

Mauritius
Mauricio
mahw-REE-thyoh

Liberia
Liberia
lee-BEH-ryah

Luxembourg
Luxemburgo
loo-xehm-BOOR-goh

Malawi
Malawi
mah-LAH-wee

Malta
Malta
MAHL-tah

Mexico
México
MEH-khee-koh

125

Micronesia
Micronesia
mee-kroh-NEH-syah

Montenegro
Montenegro
mohn-teh-NEH-groh

Nauru
Nauru
nah-OO-roo

Nicaragua
Nicaragua
nee-kah-RAH-gwah

Oman
Omán
oh-MAHN

Moldova
Moldavia
mohl-DAH-byah

Morocco
Marruecos
mah-RRWEH-kohs

Nepal
Nepal
neh-PAHL

Niger
Níger
NEE-khehr

Pakistan
Pakistán
pah-kees-TAHN

Monaco
Mónaco
MOH-nah-koh

Mozambique
Mozambique
moh-thahm-BEE-keh

Netherlands
Países Bajos
pah-EE-sehs BAH-khohs

Nigeria
Nigeria
nee-KHEH-ryah

Palau
Palaos
pah-LAHW

Mongolia
Mongolia
mohn-GOH-lyah

Namibia
Namibia
nah-MEE-byah

New Zealand
Nueva Zelanda
NWEH-bah theh-LAHN-dah

Norway
Noruega
nohr-WEH-gah

Palestinian Territories
Territorios Palestinos
teh-rree-TOH-ryohs
pah-lehs-TEE-nohs

Panama
Panamá
pah-nah-MAH

Peru
Perú
peh-ROO

Qatar
Qatar
kah-TAHR

Saint Lucia
Santa Lucía
SAHN-tah loo-THEE-yah

Senegal
Senegal
seh-neh-GAHL

Papua New Guinea
Papúa Nueva Guinea
pah-POO-ah NWEH-bah
gea-NEH-ah

Philippines
Filipinas
fee-lee-PEE-nahs

Romania
Rumanía
rroo-mah-NEE-yah

Samoa
Samoa
sah-MOH-ah

Serbia
Serbia
SEHR-byah

Paraguay
Paraguay
pah-rah-GWAY

Poland
Polonia
poh-LOH-nyah

Russia
Rusia
RROO-syah

San Marino
San Marino
sahn mah-REE-noh

Seychelles
Seychelles
sey-CHEH-lehs

Portugal
Portugal
pohr-too-GAHL

Rwanda
Ruanda
rroo-AHN-dah

Saudi Arabia
Arabia Saudí
ah-RAH-byah
sahw-THEE

Sierra Leone
Sierra Leona
SYEH-rrah leh-OH-nah

Singapore
Singapur
seen-gah-POOR

Solomon Islands
Islas Salomón
EES-lahs sah-loh-MOHN

Sri Lanka
Sri Lanka
sree LAHN-kah

Swaziland
Suazilandia
swah-thee-LAHN-thyah

Taiwan
Taiwán
tay-WAHN

Sint Maarten
Sint Maarten
seen MAHR-tehn

Somalia
Somalia
soh-MAH-lyah

Sudan
Sudán
soo-THAN

Sweden
Suecia
SWEH-thyah

Tajikistan
Tayikistán
tah-ee-kees-TAHN

Slovakia
Eslovaquia
ehs-loh-BAH-kyah

South Africa
Sudáfrica
soo-THAH-free-kah

South Sudan
Sudán del Sur
soo-THAN dehl SOOR

Switzerland
Suiza
SWEE-thah

Tanzania
Tanzania
tahn-THAH-nyah

Slovenia
Eslovenia
ehs-loh-BEH-nyah

Spain
España
ehs-PAH-nyah

Suriname
Surinam
soo-ree-NAHM

Syria
Siria
SEE-ryah

Thailand
Tailandia
tay-LAHN-dyah

Togo
Togo
TOH-goh

Turkey
Turquía
toor-KEE-yah

Ukraine
Ucrania
oo-KRAH-nyah

Uruguay
Uruguay
oo-roo-GWAY

Vietnam
Vietnam
byeth-NAHM

Tonga
Tonga
TOHN-gah

Turkmenistan
Turkmenistán
toork-meh-nees-TAHN

United Arab Emirates
Emiratos Árabes Unidos
eh-mee-RAH-tohs
AH-rah-behs oo-NEE-thohs

Uzbekistan
Uzbekistán
ooth-beh-kees-TAHN

Yemen
Yemen
yeh-MEHN

Trinidad and Tobago
Trinidad y Tobago
tree-nee-THATH ee toh-BAH-goh

Tuvalu
Tuvalu
too-BAH-loo

United Kingdom
Reino Unido
RREY-noh oo-NEE-thoh

Vanuatu
Vanuatu
bah-noo-AH-too

Zambia
Zambia
THAHM-byah

Tunisia
Túnez
TOO-neth

Uganda
Uganda
oo-GAHN-dah

United States of America
Estados Unidos de América
ehs-TAH-thohs oo-NEE-
thohs deh ah-MEH-ree-kah

Venezuela
Venezuela
beh-neh-THWEH-lah

Zimbabwe
Zimbabue
theem-BAH-bweh

129

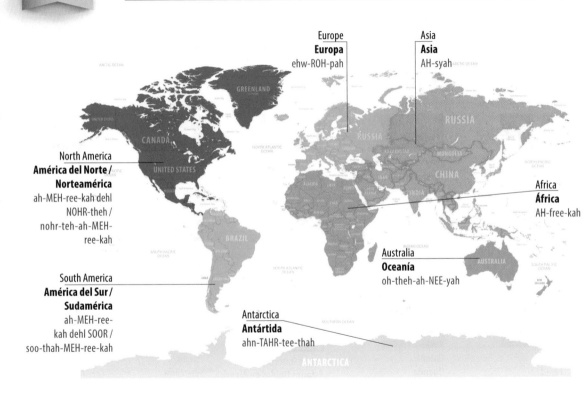

Europe
Europa
ehw-ROH-pah

Asia
Asia
AH-syah

North America
América del Norte /
Norteamérica
ah-MEH-ree-kah dehl
NOHR-theh /
nohr-teh-ah-MEH-
ree-kah

Africa
África
AH-free-kah

Australia
Oceanía
oh-theh-ah-NEE-yah

South America
América del Sur /
Sudamérica
ah-MEH-ree-
kah dehl SOOR /
soo-thah-MEH-ree-kah

Antarctica
Antártida
ahn-TAHR-tee-thah

bus stop
la parada del autobús
lah pah-RAH-thah dehl ahw-toh-BOOS

platform
el andén
ehl ahn-DEHN

(aero)plane
el avión
ehl ah-BYOHN

moped / scooter
el ciclomotor
ehl thee-kloh-moh-TOHR

(bi)cycle
la bicicleta
lah bee-thee-KLEH-tah

boat
el barco
ehl BAHR-koh

bus
el autobús
ehl ahw-toh-BOOS

ship
el barco
ehl BAHR-koh

car
el coche
ehl KOH-cheh

helicopter
el helicóptero
ehl eh-lee-KOHP-teh-roh

lorry
el camión
ehl kah-MYOHN

tanker
el petrolero
ehl peh-troh-LEH-roh

kid's scooter
el patinete
ehl pah-tee-NEH-teh

(motor)bike
la moto / la motocicleta
lah MOH-toh / lah moh-toh-thee-KLEH-tah

train
el tren
ehl trehn

taxi
el taxi
ehl TAH-ksee

ferry
el ferry
ehl FEH-rree

submarine / sub
el submarino
ehl soob-mah-REE-noh

sailing boat
el barco de vela
ehl BAHR-koh deh BEH-lah

tram
el tranvía
ehl trahn-BEE-yah

by air	**en avión**	ehn ah-BYOHN	in the port	**en el puerto**	ehn ehl PWEHR-toh
on the motorway	**en la autopista**	ehn lah ahw-toh-PEES-tah	by rail	**en tren**	ehn trehn
on the road	**en el camino**	ehn ehl kah-MEE-noh	by tube / underground	**en metro**	ehn MEH-troh
by sea	**por vía marítima**	pohr BEE-yah mah-REE-tee-mah	on foot	**a pie**	ah pyeh

airport
el aeropuerto
ehl ah-eh-roh-PWEHR-toh

arrivals
llegadas
yeh-GAH-thahs

departures
salidas
sah-LEE-thahs

luggage
el equipaje
ehl eh-kee-PAH-kheh

carry-on luggage
el equipaje de mano
ehl eh-kee-PAH-kheh deh
MAH-noh

oversized baggage
el equipaje de gran tamaño
ehl eh-kee-PAH-kheh deh grahn
tah-MAH-nyoh

check-in desk
el mostrador de facturación
ehl mohs-trah-THOHR deh
fahk-too-rah-THYOHN

customs
la aduana
lah ah-DWAH-nah

baggage reclaim
la recogida de equipaje
lah rreh-koh-KHEE-thah
deh eh-kee-PAH-kheh

boarding pass
la tarjeta de embarque
lah tahr-KHEH-tah deh
ehm-BAHR-keh

flight ticket
el billete de avión
ehl bee-YEH-teh deh ah-BYOHN

economy class
la clase turista
lah KLAH-seh too-REES-tah

business class
la primera clase
lah pree-MEH-rah KLAH-seh

arrivals lounge
la sala de llegada
lah SAH-lah deh yeh-GAH-dah

delayed
con retraso
kohn reh-TRAH-soh

to board a plane
embarcar en el avión
ehm-bahr-KAHR ehn ehl ah-BYOHN

gate
la puerta de embarque
lah PWEHR-tah deh ehm-BAHR-keh

passport
el pasaporte
ehl pah-sah-POHR-teh

passport control
el control de pasaportes
ehl kohn-TROHL deh
pah-sah-POHR-tehs

security check
el control de seguridad
ehl kohn-TROHL deh
seh-goo-ree-THATH

airline	**la compañía aérea**	lah kohm-pah-NEE-yah ah-EH-reh-ah	long-haul flight	**el vuelo de largo recorrido**	ehl BWEH-loh deh LAHR-goh rreh-koh-RREE-thoh
boarding time	**la hora de embarque**	lah OH-rah deh ehm-BAHR-keh			
charter flight	**el (vuelo) chárter**	ehl (BWEH-loh) CHAHR-tehr	The flight has been delayed.	**El vuelo se ha retrasado.**	ehl BWEH-loh seh ah rreh-trah-SAH-thoh
on time	**puntualmente**	poon-twahl-MEHN-teh			
one-way ticket	**el billete de ida**	ehl bee-YEH-teh deh EE-thah	to book a ticket to…	**reservar un billete para…**	rreh-sehr-BAHR oon bee-YEH-teh PAH-rah…
return ticket	**el billete de ida y vuelta**	ehl bee-YEH-teh deh EE-thah ee BWEHL-tah			

railway station
la estación de trenes
lah ehs-tah-THYOHN
deh TREH-nehs

train
el tren
el trehn

platform
el andén
el ahn-DEHN

express train	el tren expreso	ehl trehn ehks-PREH-soh
to get on the train	subir al tren	soo-BEER ahl trehn
to get off the train	salir del tren	sah-LEER dehl trehn
to miss a train	perder el tren	pehr-DEHR ehl trehn

train driver
el/lah maquinista
ehl/lah mah-kee-NEES-tah

travelcard
la tarjeta de viaje
lah tahr-KHEH-tah deh BYAH-kheh

train journey
el viaje en tren
ehl BYAH-kheh ehn trehn

carriage
el coche / el vagón
ehl KOH-cheh / ehl bah-GOHN

seat
el asiento
ehl ah-SYEHN-toh

station
la estación
lah ehs-tah-THYOHN

restaurant car
el coche comedor
ehl KOH-cheh koh-meh-THOHR

sleeper train
el tren nocturno
ehl trehn nohk-TOOR-noh

toilet
el baño / el aseo
ehl BAH-nyoh / ehl ah-SEH-oh

coach
el autobús
ehl ahw-toh-BOOS

bus driver
el conductor de autobús
ehl kohn-dook-TOHR deh
ahw-toh-BOOS

bus stop
la parada de autobús
lah pah-RAH-thah deh ahw-toh-BOOS

validator
la máquina validadora
lah MAH-kee-nah
bah-lee-thah-THOH-rah

double-decker bus
el autobús de dos pisos
ehl ahw-toh-BOOS deh
dohs PEE-sohs

bus journey
el viaje en autobús
ehl BYAH-kheh ehn ahw-toh-BOOS

coach station
la estación de autobuses
lah ehs-tah-THYOHN deh
ahw-toh-BOO-sehs

request stop
la parada opcional
lah pah-RAH-thah
ohp-thyoh-NAHL

bus fare	**el billete de autobús**	el bee-YEH-teh deh ahw-toh-BOOS
the next stop	**la parada siguiente**	lah pah-RAH-thah see-GYEHN-teh
night bus	**el autobús nocturno**	el ahw-toh-BOOS nohk-TOOR-noh
request stop	**la parada opcional**	la pah-RAH-dah op-thee-oh-NAHL
to get on the bus	**subir al autobús**	soo-BEER ahl ahw-toh-BOOS
to get off the bus	**salir del autobús**	sah-LEER dehl ahw-toh-BOOS
to miss a bus	**perder el autobús**	pehr-DEHR ehl ahw-toh-BOOS

hotel
el hotel
ehl oh-TEHL

campsite
la zona de acampada
lah THOH-nah deh
ah-kamh-PAH-thah

holiday resort
el complejo turístico
ehl kohm-PLEH-khoh
too-rees-TEE-koh

youth hostel
el hostal para jóvenes
ehl ohs-TAHL PAH-rah
KHOH-beh-nehs

accommodation	**el alojamiento**	ehl ah-loh-khah-MYEHN-toh
all-inclusive	**todo incluido**	TOH-thoh een-kloo-EE-thoh
half-board	**la media pensión**	lah MEH-thyah pehn-SYOHN
full-board	**la pensión completa**	lah pehn-SYOHN kohm-PLEH-tah
self-catering	**con cocina**	kohn koh-THEE-nah
Can you recommend a hotel?	**¿Puedes recomendarme un hotel?**	PWEH-thehs rreh-koh-mehn-DAHR-meh oon oh-TEHL?
We are staying at the hotel "XZ".	**Nos alojamos en el hotel "XZ".**	nohs ah-loh-KHAH-mohs ehn ehl oh-TEHL "XZ"
Have you already booked the hotel?	**¿Has ya reservado el hotel?**	ahs yah rreh-sehr-BAH-thoh ehl oh-TEHL?
I'm looking for a place to stay.	**Estoy buscando un alojamiento.**	ehs-TOY boos-KAHN-doh oon ah-loh-khah-MYEHN-toh

bed and breakfast
cama y desayuno
KAH-mah ee deh-sah-YOO-noh

single bed
la cama individual
lah KAH-mah een-dee-bee-thoo-AHL

double bed
la cama de matrimonio
lah KAH-mah deh mah-tree-MOH-nyoh

floor
el piso
ehl PEE-soh

front desk / reception
la recepción
lah rreh-thep-THYOHN

hotel manager
el director *m* / la directora *f* del hotel
ehl dee-rehk-TOHR /
lah dee-rehk-TOH-rah dehl oh-TEHL

indoor pool
la piscina cubierta
lah pees-THEE-nah koo-BYEHR-tah

key
la llave
lah YAH-beh

kitchenette
la cocina
lah koh-THEE-nah

luggage cart
el carrito de equipaje
ehl kah-RREE-toh deh eh-kee-PAH-kheh

towels
las toallas
lahs toh-AH-yahs

room service
el servicio de habitaciones
ehl sehr-BEE-thyoh de
ah-bee-tah-THYOH-nehs

139

lobby
el vestíbulo
ehl behs-TEE-boo-loh

wake-up call
el servicio de despertador
ehl sehr-BEE-thyoh deh
dehs-pehr-tah-THOHR

reservation
la reserva
lah rreh-SEHR-bah

guest
el huésped
ehl WEHS-pehth

check-in	**la facturación**	lah fahk-too-rah-THYOHN
check-out	**la salida**	lah sah-LEE-thah
complimentary breakfast	**el desayuno gratuito**	ehl deh-sah-YOO-noh grah-TWEE-toh
king-size bed	**la cama extra grande**	lah KAH-mah EHKS-trah GRAHN-deh
late charge	**el cargo por demora**	ehl KAHR-goh pohr deh-MOH-rah
full	**la máxima capacidad**	lah MAH-ksee-mah kah-pah-thee-THATH
parking pass	**el permiso de estacionamiento**	ehl pehr-MEE-soh deh EH-stah-thyoh-nah-MYEHN-toh
pay-per-view movie	**la película de pago por visión**	lah peh-LEE-koo-lah de PAH-goh pohr bee-SYOHN
queen-size bed	**la cama de matrimonio**	lah KAH-mah deh mah-tree-MOH-nyoh
rate	**la tasa**	lah TAH-sah
vacancy	**la disponibilidad**	lah dees-poh-nee-bee-lee-THATH

city-centre / downtown
el centro de la ciudad
ehl THEHN-troh deh lah thyoo-THATH

capital
la capital
lah kah-pee-TAHL

centre
el centro
ehl THEHN-troh

district
el barrio
ehl BAH-rryoh

industrial zone
la zona industrial
lah THOH-nah een-doos-TRYAHL

city
la ciudad
lah thyoo-THATH

metropolis
la metrópoli
lah meh-TROH-poh-lee

region
la región
lah rreh-KHYOHN

seaside resort
el complejo turístico costero
ehl kohm-PLEH-khoh too-REES-
tee-koh kohs-TEH-roh

141

old town
el casco antiguo
ehl KAHS-koh ahn-TEE-gwoh

ski resort
la estación de esquí
lah ehs-tah-THYOHN deh ehs-KEE

small town
una ciudad pequeña / el pueblo
OO-nah thyoo-THATH peh-KEH-nyah / ehl PWEH-bloh

suburb
el suburbio
ehl soo-BOOR-byoh

village
el pueblo
ehl PWEH-bloh

winter resort
la estación de invierno
lah ehs-tah-THYOHN deh een-BYEHR-noh

alley
el callejón
ehl kah-yeh-KHOHN

boulevard
el boulevard
ehl boo-leh-BAHR

toll road
la autopista de peaje
lah ahw-toh-PEES-tah deh peh-AH-kheh

motorway
la autopista
lah ahw-toh-PEES-tah

country road
el camino
ehl kah-MEE-noh

street
la calle
la KAH-yeh

bicycle lane
el carril bici
ehl kah-RREEL BEE-thee

bicycle path
el camino para bicicletas
ehl kah-MEE-noh PAH-rah
bee-thee-KLEH-tahs

crossroads / intersection
el cruce
ehl KROO-theh

143

traffic lights
el semáforo
ehl seh-MAH-foh-roh

red light
la luz roja
lah looth RROH-khah

orange light
la luz amarilla
lah looth ah-mah-REE-yah

green light
la luz verde
lah looth BEHR-deh

roundabout
la rotonda
lah rroh-THOHN-dah

pedestrian crossing
el paso de peatones
ehl PAH-soh deh peh-ah-TOH-nehs

pavement
la acera
lah ah-THEH-rah

bridge
el puente
ehl PWEHN-teh

footbridge
el puente peatonal
ehl PWEHN-teh peh-ah-toh-NAHL

overpass
el paso a nivel
ehl PAH-soh ah nee-BEHL

underpass
el paso subterráneo
ehl PAH-soh soob-teh-RRAH-neh-oh

tunnel
el túnel
ehl TOO-nehl

road
la carretera
lah kah-rreh-TEH-rah

street corner
la esquina de la calle
lah ehs-KEE-nah deh lah KAH-yeh

one-way street
la calle de sentido único
lah KAH-yeh deh sehn-TEE-thoh OO-nee-koh

two-lane road	**la carretera convencional**	lah kah-rreh-THE-rah kohn-behn-THYOH-nahl
fast lane	**el carril rápido**	ehl kah-RREEL RRAH-pee-thoh
left lane	**el carril izquierdo**	ehl kah-RREEL eeth-KYEHR-doh
right lane	**el carril de derecho**	el cah-RREEL deh-REH-tchoh
breakdown lane	**el arcén**	el ahr-THEHN

attractions
las atracciones turísticas
lahs ah-trahk-THYOH-nehs
too-REES-tee-kahs

casino
el casino
ehl kah-SEE-noh

guide book
la guía
lah GEA-yah

park
el parque
ehl PAHR-keh

guided tour
el tour guiado
ehl toor gea-YAH-thoh

information
la información
lah een-fohr-mah-THYOHN

itinerary
la ruta
lah RROO-tah

ruins
las ruinas
lahs rroo-EE-nahs

monument
el monumento
ehl moh-noo-MEHN-toh

museum
el museo
ehl moo-SEH-oh

national park
el parque nacional
ehl PAHR-keh nah-thyoh-NAHL

sightseeing
el turismo
ehl too-REES-moh

souvenirs
los souvenirs
lohs soo-beh-NEERS

tour bus
el autobús turístico
ehl ahw-toh-BOOS too-REES-tee-koh

tourist
el turista *m* / la turista *f*
ehl too-REES-tah / lah too-REES-tah

entrance fee / price	**el precio de la entrada**	ehl PREH-thyoh deh lah ehn-TRAH-thah
to buy a souvenir	**comprar un souvenir**	kohm-PRAHR oon soo-beh-NEER
to do a tour	**hacer un recorrido**	ah-THEHR oon rreh-koh-RREE-thoh
tour guide	**el guía turístico**	ehl GEA-yah too-REES-tee-koh

airport
el aeropuerto
ehl ah-eh-roh-PWEHR-toh

bank
el banco
ehl BAHN-koh

bus stop
la parada de autobús
lah pah-RAH-thah deh ahw-toh-BOOS

church
la iglesia
lah ee-GLEH-syah

cinema
el cine
ehl THEE-neh

city / town hall
el ayuntamiento
ehl ah-yoon-tah-MYEHN-toh

department store
los grandes almacenes
lohs GRAHN-dehs ahl-mah-THEH-nehs

factory
la fábrica
lah FAH-bree-kah

fire station
los bomberos
lohs bohm-BEH-rohs

hospital
el hospital
ehl ohs-pee-TAHL

hotel
el hotel
ehl oh-TEHL

library
la biblioteca
lah bee-blyoh-TEH-kah

theatre
el teatro
ehl teh-AH-troh

museum
el museo
ehl moo-SEH-oh

parking area
el aparcamiento
ehl ah-pahr-kah-MYEHN-toh

playground
el patio de recreo
ehl PAH-tyoh deh rreh-KREH-oh

police station
la policía
lah poh-lee-THEE-yah

post office
la oficina de correos
lah oh-fee-THEE-nah deh koh-RREH-ohs

prison
la prisión
lah pree-SYOHN

restaurant
el restaurante
ehl reh-stahw-RAHN-teh

school
la escuela
lah ehs-KWEH-lah

taxi stand
la parada de taxis
lah pah-RAH-thah deh TAH-ksees

harbour
el puerto
ehl PWEHR-toh

square
la plaza
lah PLAH-thah

supermarket
el supermercado
ehl soo-pehr-mehr-KAH-thoh

railway station
la estación de trenes
lah ehs-tah-THYOHN deh
TREH-nehs

How do I get to the railway station?	**¿Cómo llego a la estación de trenes?**	KOH-moh YEH-goh ah lah ehs-tah-THYOHN deh TREH-nehs?
Where can I find a taxi?	**¿Dónde puedo encontrar un taxi?**	DOHN-deh PWEH-thoh ehn-kohn-TRAHR oon TAH-ksee?

snorkel
el tubo de buceo
ehl TOO-boh deh
boo-THEH-oh

diving mask
la máscara de buceo
lah MAHS-kah-rah deh boo-THEH-oh

swimming goggles
las gafas de natación
lahs GAH-fahs deh
nah-tah-THYOHN

beach ball
la pelota de playa
lah peh-LOH-tah deh PLAH-yah

hat
el sombrero
ehl sohm-BREH-roh

sunglasses
las gafas de sol
lahs GAH-fahs deh sohl

sunscreen
el protector solar
ehl proh-tehk-TOHR soh-LAHR

beach towel
la toalla de playa
lah toh-AH-yah deh PLAH-yah

beach
la playa
la PLAH-yah

sun lounger
la tumbona
lah toom-BOH-nah

swimming cap	**el gorro de baño**	ehl GOH-rroh deh BAH-nyoh
bikini	**el bikini**	ehl bee-KEE-nee
swimming costume	**el traje de baño**	ehl TRAH-kheh deh BAH-nyoh
to sunbathe	**tomar el sol**	toh-MAHR ehl sohl
to swim	**nadar**	nah-THAHR

HEALTH

medicines
**las medicinas /
los medicamentos**
lahs meh-dee-THEE-nahs /
lohs meh-dee-kah-MEHN-tohs

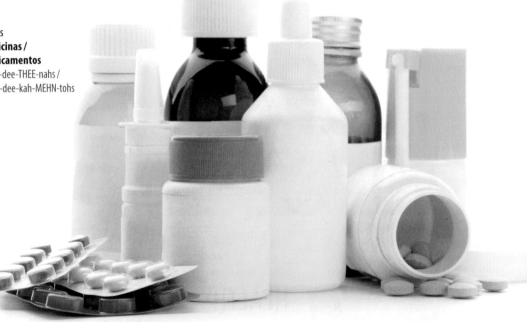

eye drops
el colirio
ehl koh-LEE-ryoh

painkiller
el analgésico
ehl ah-nahl-KHEH-see-koh

syrup
el jarabe
ehl khah-RAH-beh

to take medicine
tomar medicamentos
toh-MAHR meh-dee-kah-MEHN-tohs

shot / injection
la inyección
lah een-yehk-THYOHN

sleeping pill
el somnífero
ehl sohm-NEE-feh-roh

plaster
la tirita
lah tee-REE-tah

syringe
la jeringa
lah kheh-REEN-gah

gauze
la gasa
lah GAH-sah

pill
la pastilla
lah pahs-TEE-yah

tablet
la tableta
lah tah-BLEH-tah

ointment
la pomada
la poh-MAH-thah

155

hospital
el hospital
ehl ohs-pee-TAHL

nurse
el enfermero *m* / la enfermera *f*
ehl ehn-fehr-MEH-roh / lah ehn-fehr-MEH-rah

doctor / physician
el médico *m* / la médica *f*
ehl MEH-thee-koh / lah MEH-thee-kah

operation / surgery
la operación
lah oh-peh-rah-THYOHN

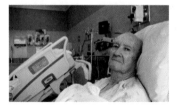

patient
el paciente *m* / la paciente *f*
ehl pah-THYEHN-theh / lah pah-THYEHN-theh

waiting room
la sala de espera
lah SAH-lah deh ehs-PEH-rah

check-up	**la revisión**	lah rreh-bee-SYOHN
diagnosis	**el diagnóstico**	ehl dyahk-NOHS-tee-koh
pharmacy /chemist's	**la farmacia**	lah fahr-MAH-thyah

prescription	**la receta**	lah rreh-THEH-tah
specialist	**el/la especialista**	ehl/lah ehs-peh-thyah-LEES-tah
treatment	**el tratamiento**	ehl trah-tah-MYEHN-toh

allergist
el alergólogo m / la alergóloga f
ehl ah-lehr-GOH-loh-goh /
lah ah-lehr-GOH-loh-gah

dentist
el dentista m / la dentista f
ehl dehn-TEES-tah /
lah dehn-TEES-tah

gynecologist
el ginecólogo m / la ginecóloga f
ehl khe-neh-KOH-loh-goh /
lah khe-neh-KOH-loh-gah

pediatrician
el pediatra m / la pediatra f
ehl peh-DYAH-trah /
lah peh-DYAH-trah

physiotherapist
el fisioterapeuta m / la fisioterapeuta f
ehl fee-syoh-theh-rah-PEHW-tah /
lah fee-syoh-theh-rah-PEHW-tah

midwife
el comadrón m / la comadrona f
ehl koh-mah-DROHN /
la koh-mah-DROH-nah

ophthalmologist
el oftalmólogo m / la oftalmóloga f
ehl ohf-tahl-MOH-loh-goh /
lah ohf-tahl-MOH-loh-gah

surgeon
el cirujano m / la cirujana f
ehl thee-roo-KHAH-noh /
lah thee-roo-KHAH-nah

anaesthesiologist	**el anestesiólogo m / la anestesióloga f**	ehl ah-nehs-teh-SYOH-loh-goh / lah ah-nehs-teh-SYOH-loh-gah
cardiologist	**el cardiólogo m / la cardióloga f**	ehl kahr-DYOH-loh-goh / lah kahr-DYOH-loh-gah
dermatologist	**el dermatólogo m / la dermatóloga f**	ehl dehr-mah-TOH-loh-goh / lah dehr-mah-TOH-loh-gah
neurologist	**el neurólogo m / la neuróloga f**	ehl nehw-ROH-loh-goh / lah nehw-ROH-loh-gah
oncologist	**el oncólogo m / la oncóloga f**	ehl ohn-KOH-loh-goh / lah ohn-KOH-loh-gah
psychiatrist	**el psiquiatra m / la psiquiatra f**	ehl see-KYAH-trah / lah see-KYAH-trah
radiologist	**el radiólogo m / la radióloga f**	ehl rrah-DYOH-loh-ghoh / lah rrah- DYOH-loh-ghah

to feel good
sentirse bien
sehn-TEER-seh byehn

to catch a cold
resfriarse
rehs-FRYAHR-seh

to have a cold
tener un resfriado
teh-NEHR oon rehs-FRYAH-thoh

to sneeze
estornudar
ehs-tohr-noo-THAHR

to cough
toser
toh-SEHR

to blow one's nose
sonarse la nariz
soh-NAHR-seh lah nah-REETH

to feel sick
sentirse mal
sehn-TEER-seh mahl

to faint
desmayarse
dehs-mah-YAHR-seh

to pass out
desmayarse
dehs-mah-YAHR-seh

to be tired
estar cansado
ehs-TAHR kahn-SAH-thoh

to be exhausted
estar agotado
ehs-TAHR ah-goh-TAH-thoh

to have back pain
tener dolor de espalda
teh-NEHR doh-LOHR deh
ehs-PAHL-dah

to have earache
tener dolor de oído
teh-NEHR doh-LOHR deh
oh-EE-thoh

to have a headache
tener dolor de cabeza
teh-NEHR doh-LOHR deh
kah-BEH-thah

to have a sore throat
tener dolor de garganta
teh-NEHR doh-LOHR deh
gahr-GAHN-tah

to have toothache
tener dolor de muelas
teh-NEHR doh-LOHR deh
MWEH-lahs

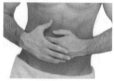
to have a stomach ache
tener dolor de estómago
teh-NEHR doh-LOHR deh
ehs-TOH-mah-goh

to have a temperature
tener fiebre
teh-NEHR FYEHB-reh

to have diarrhoea
tener diarrea
teh-NEHR dyah-RREH-ah

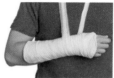
to break an arm
romperse el brazo
rrohm-PEHR-seh ehl BRAH-thoh

to be constipated
tener estreñimiento
teh-NEHR ehs-treh-nee-
MYEHN-toh

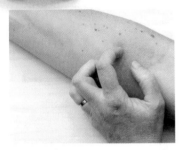

to have a rash
tener una erupción cutánea
teh-NEHR OO-nah eh-roop-THYOHN
koo-TAH-neh-ah

to be allergic to
ser alérgico a
sehr ah-LEHR-khee-koh ah

to vomit
vomitar
boh-mee-TAHR

to hurt
dañar
dah-NYAHR

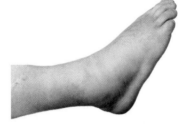

to swell
inflamarse
een-flah-MAHR-seh

to suffer from
sufrir de algo
soof-REER deh AHL-goh

chicken pox
la varicela
lah bah-ree-THEH-lah

runny nose
el catarro
ehl kah-TAH-rroh

heart attack
el ataque al corazón
ehl ah-TAH-keh ahl koh-rah-THOHN

cough
la tos
lah tohs

diarrhoea
la diarrea
lah dyah-RREH-ah

fever
la fiebre
lah FYEHB-reh

headache
el dolor de cabeza
ehl doh-LOHR deh kah-BEH-thah

injury
la lesión
lah leh-SYOHN

sore throat
el dolor de garganta
ehl doh-LOHR deh gahr-GAHN-tah

asthma
el asma
ehl AHS-mah

flu
la gripe
lah GREE-peh

health
la salud
lah sah-LOOTH

hepatitis
la hepatitis
lah eh-pah-TEE-tees

heart disease
la enfermedad del corazón
lah ehn-fehr-meh-THATH dehl koh-rah-THOHN

stomach ache
el dolor abdominal
ehl doh-LOHR ahb-doh-mee-NAHL

mouth ulcer
la úlcera de la boca
lah OOL-theh-rah deh lah BOH-kah

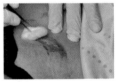

wound
la herida
lah eh-REE-thah

common cold	el resfriado común	ehl rrehs-FRYAH-thoh koh-MOON
fracture	la fractura	lah frahk-TOO-rah
illness	la enfermedad	lah ehn-fehr-meh-THATH
mumps	las paperas	lahs pah-PEH-rahs

pain	el dolor	ehl doh-LOHR
painful	doloroso	doh-loh-ROH-soh
painless	sin dolor	seen doh-LOHR
to be ill	estar enfermo	ehs-TAHR ehn-FEHR-moh

emergency number
el número de emergencia
ehl NOO-meh-roh deh eh-mehr-KHEHN-thyah

firefighter
el bombero *m* / la bombera *f*
ehl bohm-BEH-roh / lah bohm-BEH-rah

policeman
el policía *m* / la policía *f*
ehl poh-lee-THEE-yah / lah poh-lee-THEE-yah

fire engine
el camión de bomberos
ehl kah-MYOHN deh bohm-BEH-rohs

police car
el coche de policía
ehl KOH-cheh deh poh-lee-THEE-yah

ambulance
la ambulancia
lah ahm-boo-LAHN-thyah

accident
el accidente
ehl ahk-thee-THEHN-teh

paramedics
los paramédicos
lohs pah-rah-MEH-thee-kohs

emergency
la emergencia
lah eh-mehr-KHEHN-thyah

fire
el fuego
ehl FWEH-goh

patient
el paciente *m* / la paciente *f*
ehl pah-THYEHN-theh / lah pah-THYEHN-theh

police
la policía
lah poh-lee-THEE-yah

SPORT

badminton racket
la raqueta de bádminton
lah rrah-KEH-tah deh BAHD-meen-tohn

ball
el balón
ehl bah-LOHN

baseball
la pelota de béisbol
lah peh-LOH-tah deh BEYHS-bohl

bicycle
la bicicleta
lah bee-thee-KLEH-tah

bowling ball
la bola de bolos
lah BOH-lah deh BOH-lohs

cap
la gorra
lah GOH-rrah

football
el balón de fútbol
ehl bah-LOHN deh FOOT-bohl

glove
el guante
ehl GWAHN-teh

net
la red
lah rreth

goggles
las gafas de esquí
lahs GAH-fahs deh ehs-KEE

golf ball
la bola de golf
lah BOH-lah deh golf

helmet
el casco
ehl KAHS-koh

goal
la portería
lah pohr-teh-REE-yah

lane
el carril
ehl kah-RREEL

hockey puck
el disco de hockey
ehl DEES-koh deh HOH-kee

hockey stick
el palo de hockey
ehl PAH-loh deh HOH-kee

saddle
la silla de montar
lah SEE-yah deh mohn-TAHR

ice-skates
los patines
lohs pah-TEE-nehs

skates
los patines
lohs pah-TEE-nehs

ski poles
los bastones de esquí
lohs bahs-TOH-nehs deh ehs-KEE

167

skis
los esquís
lohs ehs-KEES

snowboard
la tabla de snowboard
lah TAH-blah deh snohw-BOHR

surfboard
la tabla de surf
lah TAH-blah deh soorf

squash racket
la raqueta de squash
lah rrah-KEH-tah deh skwahsh

swimming costume
el traje de baño
ehl TRAH-kheh deh BAH-nyoh

tennis ball
la pelota de tenis
lah peh-LOH-tah deh TEH-nees

tennis racket
la raqueta de tenis
lah rrah-KEH-tah deh TEH-nees

volleyball
el balón de voleibol
ehl bah-LOHN deh BOH-ley-bohl

weights
las pesas
lahs PEH-sahs

baseball
el béisbol
ehl BEYHS-bohl

bowling
los bolos
lohs BOH-lohs

football
el fútbol
ehl FOOT-bohl

hiking
el excursionismo
ehl ex-koor-syoh-NEES-moh

hockey
el hockey
ehl OH-kee

cycling
el ciclismo
ehl thee-KLEES-moh

horseriding
la equitación
lah eh-kee-tah-THYOHN

running
la carrera
lah kah-RREH-rah

skating
el patinaje
ehl pah-tee-NAH-kheh

skiing
el esquí
ehl ehs-KEE

swimming
la natación
lah nah-tah-THYOHN

tennis
el tenis
ehl TEH-nees

volleyball
el voleibol
ehl BOH-ley-bohl

weightlifting
el levantamiento de pesas
ehl leh-bahn-tah-MYEHN-toh deh PEH-sahs

basketball court
la cancha de baloncesto
lah KAHN-chah deh
bah-lohn-THEHS-toh

boxing ring
el ring de boxeo
ehl rreen deh boh-XEH-oh

golf course
el campo de golf
ehl KAHM-poh deh golf

fitness centre
el gimnasio
ehl kheem-NAH-syoh

football pitch
el campo de fútbol
ehl KAHM-poh deh FOOT-bohl

football ground
el campo de fútbol
ehl KAHM-poh deh FOOT-bohl

golf club
el club de golf
ehl KLOOB deh golf

gym
el gimnasio
ehl kheem-NAH-syoh

playground
el parque infantil
ehl PAHR-keh een-fahn-TEEL

171

racecourse
el hipódromo
ehl ee-POH-droh-moh

race track
la pista de carreras
lah PEES-tah deh kah-RREH-rahs

recreation area
la zona de recreo
lah THOH-nah deh rreh-KREH-oh

skating rink
la pista de patinaje
lah PEES-tah deh pah-tee-NAH-kheh

sports ground
el campo de deportes
ehl KAHM-poh deh deh-POHR-tehs

stadium
el estadio
ehl ehs-TAH-thyoh

swimming pool
la piscina
lah pees-THEE-nah

tennis club
el club de tenis
ehl KLOOB deh TEH-nees

tennis court
la pista de tenis
lah PEES-tah deh TEH-nees

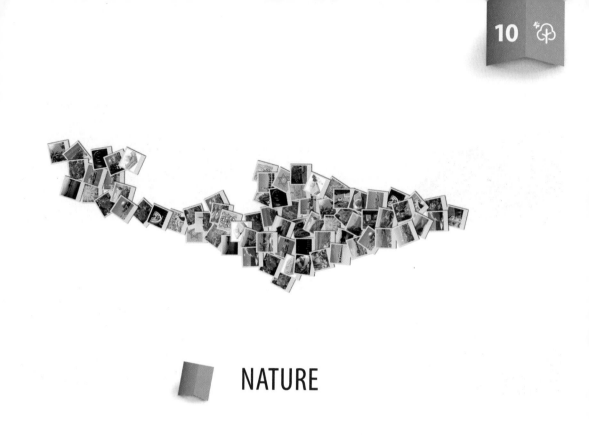

NATURE

landscape
el paisaje
ehl pay-SAH-kheh

bay
la bahía
lah bah-EE-yah

beach
la playa
lah PLAH-yah

cave
la cueva
lah KWEH-bah

stream
el arroyo
ehl ah-RROH-yoh

desert
el desierto
ehl deh-SYEHR-toh

forest   woods
el bosque **el bosque**
ehl BOHS-keh BOHS-keh

hill
la colina
lah koh-LEE-nah

earth
la tierra
lah TYEH-rrah

island
la isla
lah EES-lah

lake
el lago
ehl LAH-goh

mountain
la montaña
lah mohn-TAH-nyah

ocean
el océano
ehl oh-THEH-ah-noh

175

peak
la cumbre
lah KOOM-breh

plain
la llanura
lah yah-NOO-rah

pond
el estanque
ehl ehs-TAHN-keh

river
el río
ehl RREE-yoh

sea
el mar
ehl mahr

brook
la corriente
lah koh-RRYEHN-teh

swamp
el pantano
ehl pahn-TAH-noh

valley
el valle
ehl BAH-yeh

waterfall
la cascada
lah kahs-KAH-thah

weather
el tiempo
ehl TYEHM-poh

What's the weather like?	**¿Qué tiempo hace?**	KEH TYEHM-poh AH-theh?
What's the forecast for tomorrow?	**¿Qué tiempo hará mañana?**	KEH TYEHM-poh ah-RAH mah-NYAH-nah?

10

blizzard
la tormenta de nieve
lah tohr-MEHN-tah deh NYEH-beh

cold
frío
FREE-yoh

drizzle
la llovizna
lah yoh-BEE-thnah

flood
la inundación
lah ee-noon-dah-THYOHN

frost
la escarcha
lah ehs-KAHR-chah

humidity
la humedad
lah oo-meh-THAT

Celsius
los grados Celsius
lohs GRAH-thohs THEHL-syoos

cyclone
el ciclón
ehl thee-KLOHN

dry
seco
SEH-koh

fog
la niebla
lah NYEH-blah

hail
el granizo
ehl grah-NEE-thoh

hurricane
el huracán
ehl oo-rah-KAHN

cloud
la nube
lah NOO-beh

degree
el grado
ehl GRAH-thoh

dry season
la estación seca
lah eh-stah-THYOHN SEH-kah

forecast
la previsión
lah preh-bee-SYOHN

heat
el calor
ehl kah-LOHR

ice
el hielo
ehl YEH-loh

cloudy
nublado
noo-BLAH-thoh

dew
el rocío
ehl rroh-THEE-yoh

Fahrenheit
Fahrenheit
fah-rehn-HEYT

freeze
helar
eh-LAHR

hot
caliente
kah-LYEHN-teh

lightning
el relámpago
ehl rreh-LAHM-p

rain
la lluvia
lah YOO-byah

rainy season
la temporada de lluvias
la tehm-poh-RAH-thah
deh YOO-byahs

snowy
nevado
neh-BAH-thoh

temperature
la temperatura
lah tehm-peh-rah-TOO-rah

tsunami
el tsunami
ehl tsoo-NAH-mee

rainstorm
la tormenta
lah tohr-MEHN-tah

sleet
la aguanieve
lah ahk-wah-NYEH-beh

storm
la tormenta
lah tohr-MEHN-tah

thunder
el trueno
ehl TRWEH-noh

typhoon
el tifón
ehl tee-FOHN

windy
ventoso
behn-TOH-soh

rainbow
el arco iris
ehl AHR-koh EE-rees

snow
la nieve
lah NYEH-beh

sun
el sol
ehl sohl

thunderstorm
la tormenta
lah tohr-MEHN-tah

warm
cálido
KAH-lee-thoh

rainy
lluvioso
yoo-BYOH-soh

snowstorm
la tormenta de nieve
lah tohr-MEHN-tah
deh NYEH-beh

sunny
soleado
soh-leh-AH-thoh

tornado
el tornado
ehl tohr-NAH-thoh

wind
el viento
ehl BYEHN-toh

pet owner
el dueño *m* /
la dueña *f* **de la mascota**
ehl DWEH-nyoh /
lah DWEH-nyah deh lah mahs-KOH-tah

aquarium
el acuario
ehl ah-KWAH-ryoh

cage
la jaula
lah KHAHW-

bird
el pájaro
ehl PAH-khah-roh

dog
el perro
ehl PEH-rroh

canary
el canario
ehl kah-NAH-ryoh

cat
el gato
ehl GAH-toh

pet shop
la tienda de mascotas
lah TYEHN-dah deh mahs-KOH-tahs

fish
el pez
ehl pehth

gecko
el geco
ehl KHEH-koh

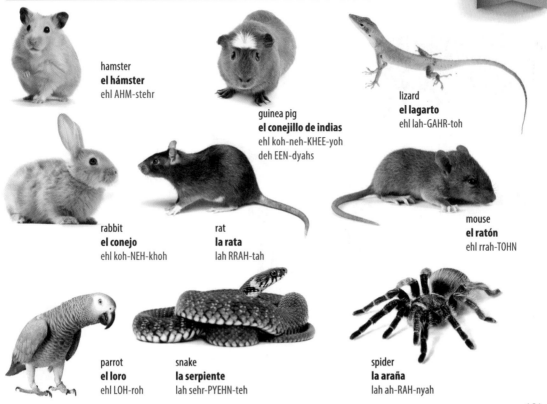

hamster
el hámster
ehl AHM-stehr

guinea pig
el conejillo de indias
ehl koh-neh-KHEE-yoh
deh EEN-dyahs

lizard
el lagarto
ehl lah-GAHR-toh

rabbit
el conejo
ehl koh-NEH-khoh

rat
la rata
lah RRAH-tah

mouse
el ratón
ehl rrah-TOHN

parrot
el loro
ehl LOH-roh

snake
la serpiente
lah sehr-PYEHN-teh

spider
la araña
lah ah-RAH-nyah

cow
la vaca
la BAH-kah

chicken
el pollo
el POH-yoh

donkey
el burro
el BOO-rroh

goose
el ganso
ehl GAHN-soh

goat
la cabra
la KAH-brah

horse
el caballo
ehl kah-BAH-yoh

sheep
la oveja
lah oh-BEH-khah

duck
el pato
el PAH-toh

rabbit
el conejo
ehl koh-NEH-khoh

pig
el cerdo
ehl THEHR-doh

turkey
el pavo
ehl PAH-boh

giraffe
la jirafa
lah khee-RAH-fah

elephant
el elefante
ehl eh-leh-FAHN-teh

jaguar
el jaguar
ehl khah-GWAHR

tiger
el tigre
ehl TEE-greh

lion
el león
ehl leh-OHN

leopard
el leopardo
ehl leh-oh-PAHR-doh

puma
el puma
ehl POO-mah

hippopotamus
el hipopótamo
ehl ee-poh-POH-tah-moh

monkey
el mono
ehl MOH-noh

chimpanzee
el chimpancé
ehl cheem-pahn-THEH

ostrich
el avestruz
ehl ah-behs-

sloth
el perezoso
ehl peh-reh-THOH-s

rhinoceros
el rinoceronte
ehl ree-noh-theh-
ROHN-teh

armadillo
el armadillo
ehl ahr-mah-THEE-yoh

iguana
la iguana
lah ee-GWAH-nah

kangaroo
el canguro
ehl kahn-GOO-roh

bear
el oso
ehl OH-soh

zebra
la cebra
lah THEH-brah

hyena
la hiena
lah YEH-nah

seal
la foca
lah FOH-kah

gazelle
la gacela
lah gah-THEH-lah

antelope
el antílope
ehl ahn-TEE-loh-peh

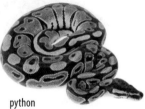

python
la serpiente pitón
lah sehr-PYEHN-teh pee-TOHN

water buffalo
el búfalo de agua
ehl BOO-fah-loh
deh AHK-wah

boar
el jabalí
ehl kha-bah-LEE

cobra
la cobra
lah KOH-brah

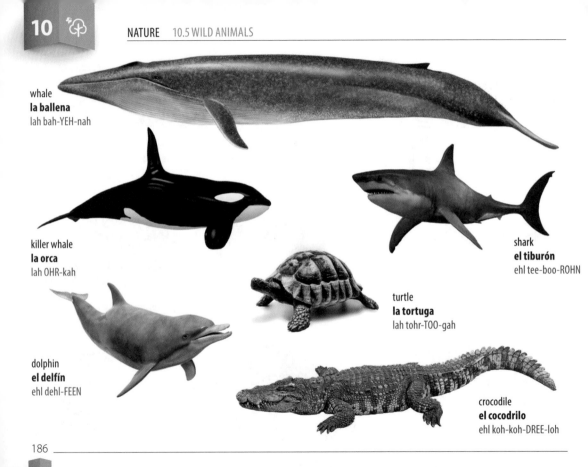

whale
la ballena
lah bah-YEH-nah

killer whale
la orca
lah OHR-kah

shark
el tiburón
ehl tee-boo-ROHN

turtle
la tortuga
lah tohr-TOO-gah

dolphin
el delfín
ehl dehl-FEEN

crocodile
el cocodrilo
ehl koh-koh-DREE-loh

 SHOPPING AND SERVICES

grocery store
la tienda de comestibles
lah TYEHN-dah deh koh-mehs-TEE-blehs

bazaar
el bazar
ehl bah-THAHR

bookshop
la librería
lah lee-breh-REE-yah

computer shop
la tienda de ordenadores
lah TYEHN-dah deh
ohr-deh-nah-THOH-rehs

corner shop
la tienda de barrio
lah TYEHN-dah deh BAH-rryoh

farmers' market
el mercado agrícola
ehl mehr-KAH-thoh ah-GREE-koh-lah

flea market
el mercadillo
ehl mehr-kah-THEE-yoh

flower market
el mercado de las flores
ehl mehr-KAH-thoh deh lahs FLOH-rehs

bakery
la panadería
lah pah-nah-theh-REE-yah

fruit stall
el puesto de frutas
ehl PWEHS-toh deh FROO-tahs

market
el mercado
ehl mehr-KAH-thoh

newsagent
el quiosco
ehl KYOHS-koh

shoe shop
la tienda de zapatos
lah TYEHN-dah deh thah-PAH-tohs

street vendor
el vendedor ambulante
ehl behn-deh-THOHR ahm-boo-LAHN-teh

supermarket
el supermercado
ehl soo-pehr-mehr-KAH-thoh

| department store | **los grandes almacenes** | los GRAHN-dehs ahl-mah-THEH-nehs |
| shopping centre | **el centro comercial** | ehl THEN-troh koh-mehr-THYAHL |

sale
las rebajas
lahs rreh-BAH-khahs

checkout / till checkout
la caja
lah KAH-khah

conveyor belt
la cinta transportadora
lah THEEN-tah trahns-pohr-tah-THOH-rah

customer
el cliente _m_ / la cliente _f_
ehl klee-YEHN-teh / lah klee-YEHN-teh

price
el precio
ehl PREH-thyoh

queue
la cola
lah KOH-lah

receipt
el ticket de compra
ehl TEE-keht deh KOHM-prah

cashier
el cajero _m_ / la cajera _f_
ehl kah-KHEH-roh / lah kah-KHEH-rah

shopping bag
la bolsa de compra
lah BOHL-sah deh KOHM-prah

shopping list
la lista de la compra
lah LEES-tah deh lah KOHM-prah

shopping basket
la cesta de la compra
lah THEHS-tah deh lah KOHM-prah

trolley
el carrito
ehl kah-RREE-toh

bill for	**la factura para**	lah fahk-TOO-rah PAH-rah
Can I help you?	**¿Puedo ayudarte?**	PWEH-thoh ah-yoo-THAHR-the?
goods	**los bienes**	lohs BYEH-nehs
shopper	**el comprador *m* / la compradora *f***	ehl kohm-prah-THOHR / lah kohm-prah-THOH-rah
to cost	**costar**	kohs-TAHR
to get a great bargain	**conseguir un gran negocio**	kohn-seh-GEAR oon grahn neh-GOH-thyoh
to purchase	**comprar**	kohm-PRAHR
to queue	**hacer cola**	ah-THEHR KOH-lah

coat
el abrigo
ehl ah-BREE-goh

belt
el cinturón
ehl theen-too-ROHN

boots
las botas
lahs BOH-tahs

hat
el sombrero
ehl sohm-BREH-roh

gloves
los guantes
lohs GWAHN-tehs

raincoat
el impermeable
ehl eem-pehr-meh-AH-bleh

jeans
los (pantalones) vaqueros
lohs (pahn-tah-LOH-nehs) bah-KEH-rohs

pyjamas
el pijama
ehl pee-KHAH-mah

jacket
la chaqueta
lah chah-KEH-tah

shoes
los zapatos
lohs thah-PAH-tohs

jumper
el jersey
ehl khehr-SEY

scarf
la bufanda
lah boo-FAHN-dah

underwear
la ropa interior
lah RROH-pah een-
theh-RYOHR

tie
la corbata
lah kohr-BAH-tah

sweatshirt
la sudadera
lah soo-thah-THEH-rah

briefs
los calzoncillos
lohs kahl-thohn-THEE-lyohs

shirt
la camisa
lah kah-MEE-sah

11

trousers
los pantalones
lohs pahn-tah-LOH-nehs

t-shirt
la camiseta
lah kah-mee-SEH-tah

socks
los calcetines
lohs kahl-theh-TEE-nehs

undershirt
la camiseta interior
lah kah-mee-SEH-tah een-teh-RYOHR

suit
el traje
ehl TRAH-kheh

slippers
las zapatillas de casa
lahs thah-pah-TEE-yahs deh KAH-sah

He has a hat on.	**Él tiene un sombrero.**	EHL TYEH-neh oon sohm-BREH-roh.
These briefs are the right size.	**Estos calzoncillos son del tamaño correcto.**	EHS-tohs kahl-thohn-THEE-lyohs sohn dehl tah-MAH-nyoh koh-RREH-ktoh
What did he have on?	**¿Qué tenía puesto él?**	KEH teh-NEE-yah PWEHS-toh EHL?
I want these boxer shorts in a size 42.	**Querría estos boxers en la talla 42 (cuarenta y dos) por favor.**	keh-RREE-yah EH-stohs BOH-xehrs ehn lah TAH-yah 42 (kwah-REHN-tah ee dohs) pohr fah-BOHR

raincoat
el impermeable
ehl eem-pehr-meh-AH-bleh

boots
las botas
lahs BOH-tahs

jacket
la chaqueta
lah chah-KEH-tah

gloves
los guantes
lohs GWAHN-tehs

hat
el sombrero
ehl sohm-BREH-roh

jeans
los (pantalones) vaqueros
lohs (pahn-tah-LOH-nehs)
bah-KEH-rohs

coat
el abrigo
ehl ah-BREE-goh

pyjamas
el pijama
ehl pee-KHAH-mah

belt
el cinturón
ehl theen-too-ROHN

195

scarf
la bufanda
la boo-FAHN-dah

jumper
el jersey
el khehr-SEY

pants
las bragas
lahs BRAH-gahs

dress
el vestido
el veh-STEE-doh

skirt
la falda
la FAHL-dah

shoes
los zapatos
los thah-PAH-tohs

sweatshirt
la sudadera
la soo-thah-THEH-rah

socks
los calcetines
los kahl-theh-TEE-nehs

shirt
la camisa
la kah-MEE-sah

stockings
las medias
lahs MEH-thyahs

suit
el traje
ehl TRAH-kheh

t-shirt
la camiseta
lah kah-mee-SEH-tah

underwear
la ropa interior
lah RROH-pah een-theh-RYOHR

trousers
los pantalones
lohs pahn-tah-LOH-nehs

slacks
los pantalones
lohs pahn-tah-LOH-nehs

bra
el sujetador
ehl soo-kheh-tah-THOHR

slippers
**las zapatillas
de casa**
lahs thah-pah-
TEE-yahs deh
KAH-sah

She has a hat on.	**Ella lleva un sombrero.**	EH-yah YEH-bah oon sohm-BREH-roh
The dress looks nice on you.	**El vestido te queda bien.**	ehl behs-TEE-thoh teh KEH-thah byehn
What did she have on?	**¿Qué tenía puesto ella?**	KEH teh-NEE-yah PWEHS-toh EH-yah?
I want these boots in a size 38.	**Quiero estas botas de número 38.**	KYEH-roh EHS-tahs BOH-tahs deh NOO-meh-roh 38

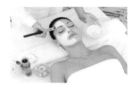

barber shop
el barbero
ehl bahr-BEH-roh

beauty salon
el salón de belleza
ehl sah-LOHN deh beh-YEH-thah

car repair shop
el taller de reparación de automóviles
ehl tah-YEHR deh rreh-pah-rah-THYOHN deh ahw-toh-MOH-bee-lehs

bicycle repair shop
el taller de bicicletas
ehl tah-YEHR deh bee-thee-KLEH-tahs

watchmaker
el relojero
ehl rre-loh-KHEH-roh

laundromat
la lavandería
lah lah-bahn-deh-REE-yah

dry cleaners
la lavandería
lah lah-bahn-deh-REE-yah

locksmiths
el cerrajero
ehl theh-rrah-KHEH-roh

petrol station
la gasolinera
lah gah-soh-lee-NEH-rah

CULTURE AND MEDIA

blog
el blog
ehl blokh

to broadcast
retransmitir
rreh-trahn-smee-TEER

magazine
la revista
lah rreh-BEES-tah

newspaper
el periódico
ehl peh-RYOH-thee-koh

radio
la radio
lah RRAH-thyoh

television
la televisión
lah teh-leh-bee-SYOHN

news broadcast
el telediario
ehl teh-leh-DYAH-ryoh

weather forecast
el pronóstico del tiempo
ehl proh-NOHS-tee-koh dehl TYEHM-poh

blogosphere	**la blogosfera**	lah bloh-goh-SFEH-rah
mass media	**los medios de comunicación**	lohs MEH-thyohs deh koh-moo-nee-kah-THYOHN
news	**las noticias**	lahs noh-TEE-thyahs
press	**la prensa**	lah PREHN-sah
tabloid	**el tabloide**	ehl tah-BLOY-theh
programme	**el programa**	ehl proh-GRAH-mah
soap	**la telenovela**	lah teh-leh-noh-BEH-lah
drama	**el drama**	ehl DRAH-mah
series	**la serie**	lah SEH-ryeh
film	**la película**	lah peh-LEE-koo-lah
documentary	**el documental**	ehl doh-koo-mehn-TAHL
music programme	**el programa de música**	ehl proh-GRAH-mah deh MOO-see-kah
sports programme	**el programa de deportes**	ehl proh-GRAH-mah deh deh-POHR-tehs
talk show	**el programa de entrevistas**	ehl proh-GRAH-mah deh ehn-treh-BEES-tahs
episode	**el episodio**	ehl eh-pee-SOH-thyoh
business news	**las noticias económicas**	lahs noh-TEE-thyahs eh-koh-NOH-mee-kahs
sports report	**la información deportiva**	lah een-fohr-mah-THYOHN deh-pohr-TEE-bah
book review	**la reseña de un libro**	lah rreh-SEH-nyah deh oon LEE-broh
ad / advertisement	**la publicidad**	lah poo-blee-thee-THATH

message
el mensaje
ehl mehn-SAH-kheh

address URL
la dirección URL
lah dee-rehk-THYOHN oo-EH-rreh-EH-leh

application / app
la aplicación
lah ah-plee-kah-THYOHN

network
la red
lah rreth

inbox	**la bandeja de entrada**	lah bahn-deh-KHAH deh ehn-TRAH-thah
IP address	**la dirección IP**	lah dee-rehk-THYOHN ee-PEH
internet	**Internet**	een-tehr-NETH
website	**el sitio web**	ehl see-TYOH web
mail	**el correo**	ehl koh-RREH-oh
search engine	**el motor de búsqueda**	ehl moh-TOHR deh BOOS-keh-thah
to search	**buscar**	boos-KAHR
to share	**compartir**	kohm-pahr-TEER
to log in	**registrarse**	rreh-khees-TRAHR-seh

to send
enviar
ehn-bee-YAHR

login
el nombre de usuario
ehl NOHM-breh deh oo-soo-AH-ryoh

to log out
finalizar sesión
fee-nah-lee-THAHR seh-SYOHN

to upload	**cargar / subir**	kahr-GAHR / soo-BEER
to download	**descargar**	dehs-kahr-GAHR
to tag	**etiquetar**	eh-tee-keh-TAHR
to comment	**comentar**	koh-mehn-TAHR
to publish	**publicar**	poo-blee-KAHR
to contact	**contactar**	kohn-tahk-TAHR
to receive	**obtener**	ohb-teh-NEHR
to add	**añadir**	ah-nyah-THEER

link
el enlace
ehl ehn-LAH-theh

CD
el CD
ehl theh-THEH

CD-ROM
el CD-ROM
ehl theh-theh-RROHM

DVD
el DVD
ehl deh-OO-beh-theh

mouse
el ratón
ehl rrah-TOHN

flash drive
la memoria USB
lah meh-MOH-ryah
oo EH-seh beh

laptop
el (ordenador) portátil
ehl (ohr-deh-nah-THOHR) pohr-TAH-teel

keyboard
el teclado
ehl teh-KLAH-thoh

modem
el módem
ehl MOH-thehm

monitor
el monitor
ehl moh-nee-TOHR

router
el router
ehl RROO-tehr

tablet
la tableta / la tablet
lah tah-BLEH-tah / lah TAH-bleht

printer
la impresora
lah eem-preh-SOH-rah

scanner
el escáner
ehl ehs-KAH-nehr

to copy	**copiar**	koh-PYAHR
to delete	**borrar**	boh-RRAHR
desktop	**el escritorio**	ehl ehs-kree-TOH-ryoh
file	**el archivo**	ehl ahr-CHEE-boh
folder	**la carpeta**	lah kahr-PEH-tah
offline	**desconectado**	dehs-koh-nehk-TAH-thoh
online	**conectado**	koh-nehk-TAH-thoh
password	**la contraseña**	lah kohn-trah-SEH-nyah

to print	**imprimir**	eem-pree-MEER
to save	**guardar**	gwahr-DAHR
to scan	**escanear**	ehs-kah-neh-AHR
screenshot	**la captura de pantalla**	lah kahp-TOO-rah deh pahn-TAH-yah
server	**el servidor**	ehl sehr-bee-THOHR
software	**el software**	ehl SOHF-wehr
to undo	**deshacer**	dehs-ah-THEHR
virus	**el virus informático**	ehl BEE-roos een-fohr-MAH-tee-koh

at
arroba
ah-RROH-bah

hash
almohadilla
ahl-moh-ah-THEE-yah

percent
porcentaje
pohr-then-TAH-kheh

circumflex
circunflejo
theer-koon-FLEH-khoh

ampersand
signo *et*
SEEG-noh *eht*

asterisk
asterisco
ahs-teh-REES-koh

tilde
tilde
TEEL-deh

tab key
tecla de tabulación
TEH-klah deh
tah-boo-lah-THYOHN

caps lock key
**tecla de bloqueo
de mayúsculas**
TEH-klah deh bloh-KEH-oh
deh mah-YOOS-koo-lahs

shift key
tecla shift (de mayúsculas)
TEH-klah shift
(deh mah-YOOS-koo-lahs)

ctrl (control) key
tecla ctrl (control)
TEH-klah ctrl (kohn-TROHL)

exclamation mark
signo de exclamación
SEEG-noh deh ex-klah-mah-THYOHN

alt (alternate) key
tecla alt (de alternativa)
TEH-klah ahlt
(deh ahl-tehr-nah-TEE-bah)

spacebar key
barra espaciadora
BAH-rrah eh-spah-thyah-THOH-rah

WIRELESS KEYBOARD K900

minus / dash
menos / guión
MEH-nohs / gea-YOHN

plus
más
mahs

equal
igual
ee-GWAHL

colon
dos puntos
dohs POON-tohs

semicolon
punto y coma
POON-toh ee KOH-mah

dot / full stop
punto
POON-toh

question mark
signo de interrogación
SEEG-noh deh
een-teh-rroh-gah-THYOHN

enter key
tecla enter (entrar)
TEH-klah enter
(ehn-TRAHR)

forward slash
barra inclinada
BAH-rrah
een-klee-NAH-thah

back slash
barra invertida
BAH-rrah
een-behr-TEE-thah

backspace key
tecla backspace
TEH-klah backspace

delete (del) key
tecla de borrar
TEH-klah deh boh-RRAHR

amusement park
el parque de atracciones
ehl PAHR-keh deh ah-trahk-THYOH-nehs

aquarium
el acuario
ehl ah-KWAH-ryoh

art gallery
la galería de arte
lah gah-leh-REE-yah deh AHR-teh

art museum
el museo de arte
ehl moo-SEH-oh deh AHR-teh

botanical garden
el jardín botánico
ehl khar-DEEN boh-TAH-nee-koh

cinema
el cine
ehl THEE-neh

circus
el circo
ehl THEER-koh

discotheque
la discoteca
lah dees-koh-TEH-kah

exhibition
la exposición
lah ex-poh-see-THYON

garden
el jardín
ehl khar-DEEN

night club
el club nocturno
ehl kloob nohk-TOOR-noh

opera house
la ópera
lah OH-peh-rah

concert hall
la sala de conciertos
lah SAH-lah deh kohn-THYEHR-tohs

park
el parque
ehl PAHR-keh

planetarium
el planetario
ehl plah-neh-TAH-ryoh

science museum
el museo de ciencia
ehl moo-SEH-oh deh THYEHN-thyah

sights
los lugares de interés
lohs loo-GAH-rehs deh een-teh-REHS

theatre
el teatro
ehl teh-AH-troh

tourist attraction
la atracción turística
lah ah-trahk-THYOHN too-REES-tee-kah

water park
el parque acuático
ehl PAHR-keh ah-KWAH-tee-koh

zoo
el parque zoológico
ehl PAHR-keh thoh-oh-LOH-khee-koh

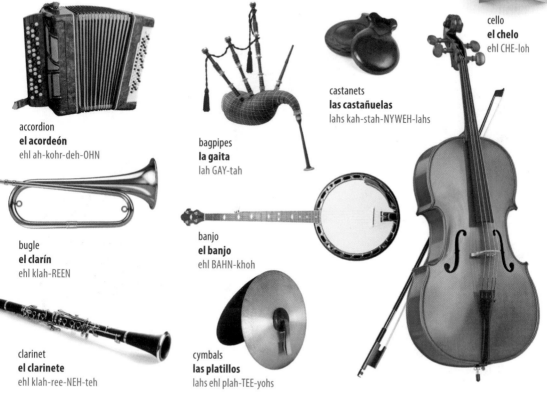

accordion
el acordeón
ehl ah-kohr-deh-OHN

bugle
el clarín
ehl klah-REEN

clarinet
el clarinete
ehl klah-ree-NEH-teh

bagpipes
la gaita
lah GAY-tah

banjo
el banjo
ehl BAHN-khoh

cymbals
las platillos
lahs ehl plah-TEE-yohs

castanets
las castañuelas
lahs kah-stah-NYWEH-lahs

cello
el chelo
ehl CHE-loh

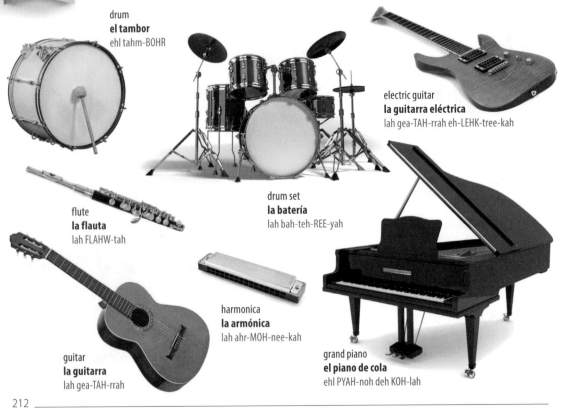

drum
el tambor
ehl tahm-BOHR

electric guitar
la guitarra eléctrica
lah gea-TAH-rrah eh-LEHK-tree-kah

flute
la flauta
lah FLAHW-tah

drum set
la batería
lah bah-teh-REE-yah

guitar
la guitarra
lah gea-TAH-rrah

harmonica
la armónica
lah ahr-MOH-nee-kah

grand piano
el piano de cola
ehl PYAH-noh deh KOH-lah

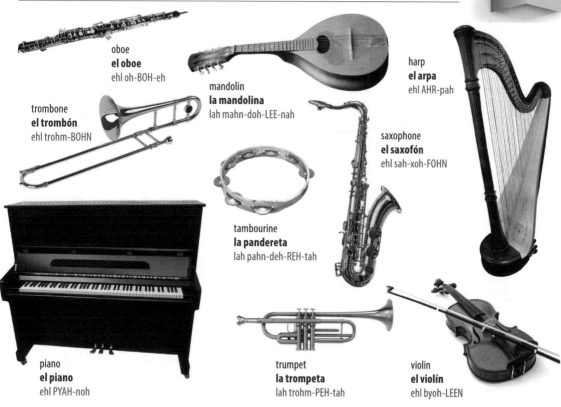

oboe
el oboe
ehl oh-BOH-eh

mandolin
la mandolina
lah mahn-doh-LEE-nah

harp
el arpa
ehl AHR-pah

trombone
el trombón
ehl trohm-BOHN

saxophone
el saxofón
ehl sah-xoh-FOHN

tambourine
la pandereta
lah pahn-deh-REH-tah

piano
el piano
ehl PYAH-noh

trumpet
la trompeta
lah trohm-PEH-tah

violin
el violín
ehl byoh-LEEN

Index

C

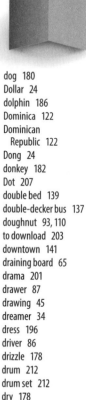

dry season 178
duck 96, 182
duplex house 56
to dust 74
dust cloth 75
dustpan 75
DVD 204

E

ear 40
earth 175
East Timor 122
Easter 51
Easter bunny 53
economy class 133
Ecuador 122
education 82
egg 94, 106
Egypt 122
eight 15
eight am 17
eight pm 17
eighteen 15
eighteenth 16
eighth 16
eightieth 16

eighty 15
El Salvador 122
elastic bands 89
electric guitar 212
elegant 27
elephant 183
eleven 15
eleven am 17
eleven pm 17
eleventh 16
email address 13, 14
embarrassed 42
emergency 164
emergency number 163
employee 83
employer 83
energetic 35
engagement 51
engineer 86
English 79
enter key 207
entrance fee 147
entrance price 147
envelope 89
episode 201

equal 207
Equatorial Guinea 122
Eritrea 122
Estonia 123
Ethiopia 123
Euro 24
Europe 130
evening 21
exchange rate 24
exchange rate for US Dollars to Japanese Yen 24
excited 42
exclamation mark 206
Excuse me, could you tell me the time please? 18
to expect a baby 39
experience 83
express train 135
expressway 145
eye 40
eye drops 155
eyebrows 32
eyelashes 32

F

face 40
face cloth 62
factory 149
Fahrenheit 178
to faint 158
family 36
family holiday 118
family with two children 38
farm 57
farmer 84
farmers' market 188
fashionable 27
fast lane 145
fat 29
father 37
Father Christmas 52
father-in-law 37
feather duster 75
February 20
to feel good 158
to feel sick 158
ferry 132
fever 161
fifteen 15

fifteenth 16
fifth 16
fiftieth 16
fifty 15
fig 98
Fiji 123
file 88, 205
filing cabinet 87
film 201
finger 41
Finland 123
fire 164
to fire 83
fire engine 163
fire station 149
firefighter 84, 163
fireworks 52
first 16
first name 12
fish 105, 180
fish and chips 113
fish sandwich 112
fisherman 84
fishing 47
fitness centre 171
five 15

five am 17
five past 18
five pm 17
five to 18
flat 56
flatshare 57
flea market 188
flight ticket 133
flood 178
floor 139
to floss your teeth 49
flower market 188
flu 162
flush 61
flute 212
fog 178
folder 205
food market 188
foot 41
footbridge 144
football 47, 166, 169
football ground 171
football pitch 171
for two months 20
forecast 178
foreign exchange 24

margarine 106
marital status 13
market 189
marks 78
marmalade 94
marriage 51
married 13
to marry 39
Marshall Islands 125
marshmallow 111
martial arts 47
mask 152
mass media 201
maternity leave 83
Mathematics 79
Mauritania 125
Mauritius 125
May 20
mayonnaise 108
meal 116
meat 97
mechanic 85
medicines 154
medium-length 31
melon 99
menu 115

Merry Christmas! 53
message 202
metropolis 141
Mexico 125
Micronesia 126
microwave 64, 73
middle-aged 26
middle-aged man 26
midnight 17
midwife 157
milk 92, 106
milkshake 111
mince 96
minus 207
mirror 61
to miss a bus 137
to miss a train 135
mistletoe 52
to mix 114
mixer 73
mixing bowl 66
mobile 72
modem 204
Moldova 126
Monaco 126
Monday 19

Mongolia 126
monitor 204
monkey 184
monkfish 105
Montenegro 126
monument 146
mop 75
moped 131
morning 21
Morocco 126
mortgage 23
mother 37
mother-in-law 37
(motor)bike 132
motorway 143
mountain 175
mountain biking 47
mouse 181, 204
mouth 40
mouth ulcer 162
Mozambique 126
muffin 110
mug 69
mumps 162
museum 146, 150
mushroom 102

Music 79
music programme 201
musician 84
mussels 104
mustard 108
My hobby is ... 44

N
nachos 112
nail clippers 63
Namibia 126
national park 146
Nauru 126
neat 27
neck 41
nectarine 100
negative 34
Nepal 126
nephew 36
net 82, 166
Netherlands 126
network 202
neurologist 157
New Year 53
New Zealand 126
news 201

news broadcast 201
newsagent 189
newspaper 200
the next stop 137
Nicaragua 126
niece 36
Niger 126
Nigeria 126
night 21
night bus 137
night club 209
nine 15
nine am 17
nine pm 17
nineteen 15
nineteenth 16
ninetieth 16
ninety 15
ninth 16
noon 17, 21
North America 130
Norway 126
nose 40
not very tall 28
notebook 80
notepad 90

notice 83
November 20
nurse 85, 156
nutmeg 108

O
obese 29
oboe 213
ocean 175
October 20
octopus 105
office 58, 87
offline 205
ointment 155
old 26
old town 142
Oman 126
omelette 94
on foot 132
on Monday 19
on the motorway 132
on the road 132
on time 134
oncologist 157
one 15
one am 17